BERLIN

GRAND STREET
69

This issue of *GRAND STREET*
is dedicated to the memory of :
ADOLFO BIOY CASARAS 1914–1999
LEO CASTELLI 1907–1999
KARL KROLOW 1915–1999 &
WILLIE MORRIS 1934–1999

Grand Street (ISSN 0734-5496; ISBN 1-885490-18-6) is published quarterly by Grand Street Press (a project of the New York Foundation for the Arts, Inc., a not-for-profit corporation), 214 Sullivan Street, Suite 6C, New York, NY 10012. Tel: (212) 533-2944, Fax: (212) 533-2737. Contributions and gifts to Grand Street Press are tax-deductible to the extent allowed by law. This publication is made possible, in part, by a grant from the New York State Council on the Arts.

Volume Eighteen, Number One (*Grand Street* 69—Summer 1999). Copyright © 1999 by the New York Foundation for the Arts, Inc., Grand Street Press. All rights reserved. Reproduction, whether in whole or in part, without permission is strictly prohibited. Second-class postage paid at New York, NY, and additional mailing offices. Postmaster: Please send address changes to Grand Street Subscription Service, Dept. GRS, P.O. Box 3000, Denville, NJ 07834. Subscriptions are $40 a year (four issues). Foreign subscriptions (including Canada) are $55 a year, payable in U.S. funds. Single-copy price is $12.95 ($18 in Canada). For subscription inquiries, please call (212) 533-2944.

Grand Street is printed by Hull Printing in Meriden, CT. It is distributed to the trade by D.A.P./Distributed Art Publishers, 155 Avenue of the Americas, New York, NY 10013, Tel: (212) 627-1999, Fax: (212) 627-9484, and to newsstands only by Bernhard DeBoer, Inc., 113 E. Centre Street, Nutley, NJ 07110, Total Circulation, 80 Frederick Street, Hackensack, NJ 07601, Ingram Periodicals, 1226 Heil Quaker Blvd., La Vergne, TN 37086, and Ubiquity Distributors, 607 Degraw Street, Brooklyn, NY 11217. *Grand Street* is distributed in Australia and New Zealand by Peribo Pty, Ltd., 58 Beaumont Road, Mount Kuring-Gai, NSW 2080, Australia, Tel: (2) 457-0011, and in the United Kingdom by Central Books, 99 Wallis Road, London E9 5LN, Tel: (181) 986-4854.

GRAND STREET

EDITOR
Jean Stein

ASSOCIATE EDITOR
Daniel Slager

ART EDITOR
Walter Hopps

MANAGING EDITOR
Tamalyn Miller

ASSOCIATE ART EDITOR
Anne Doran

POETRY EDITOR
Michael Schmidt

DESIGN
J. Abbott Miller, Scott Devendorf, Roy Brooks
PENTAGRAM, NEW YORK

ASSISTANT EDITOR
Rachel Kushner

ADMINISTRATIVE ASSISTANT
Vicky Carroll

INTERNS
Jessica Lucy Berenbeim, Ilka Saal, Sahra Webster

CONSULTING EDITORS FOR THE BERLIN ISSUE
Michi Strausfeld, Christopher Phillips

ADVISORY EDITOR
Edward W. Said

CONTRIBUTING EDITORS
George Andreou, Dominique Bourgois, Natasha Parry Brook, Frances Coady,
Mike Davis, Colin de Land, Kennedy Fraser, Jonathan Galassi, Stephen Graham,
Nikolaus Hansen, Dennis Hopper, Hudson, Jane Kramer, Brigitte Lacombe, Peter Mayer,
Charles Merewether, Michael Naumann, Erik Rieselbach, Robin Robertson, Fiona Shaw,
Robert Storr, Michi Strausfeld, Deborah Treisman, Katrina vanden Heuvel,
Wendy vanden Heuvel, John Waters, Drenka Willen

FOUNDING CONTRIBUTING EDITOR
Andrew Kopkind (1935–1994)

PUBLISHERS
Jean Stein & Torsten Wiesel

PAGES FROM THE BLACK NOTEBOOK

LÁSZLÓ DARVASI

ERNŐ SZÍV WAS OFF AGAIN. He was in Berlin, in the eastern part of the city, which he had hardly seen. Driving through after his arrival, he got the fleeting impression that by his standards it was a tremendously large city—and that this was the way it wanted to be. He was staying in Pankow, a neighborhood in the north, amid fall greenery. There were shady streets and neat villas, and there was a large, pretty park, where wooden bridges spanned shallow canals, ducklings chattered in the clear water, and lovers, sheep dogs, and baby carriages tried to get out of one another's way. On the streets the tinny clatter of pink Trabants could still be heard. He rented a flat on Majakowskiring, and for a few days he had a Polish writer as a neighbor, although after several introductions he still hadn't caught his name.

Szív turned on the television one evening and watched a documentary about the Wall. Most of the images were familiar, and showed how the Wall was built, how it had been responsible for many deaths, and the euphoria and wild celebrations when it was torn down. As Szív watched the extraordinary event replayed, he started crying; his tears flowed and wouldn't stop. A few days later he tried to explain to a Hungarian journalist who had been living in Berlin for years that freedom, after all, was the most important thing in the world. They sat in a cozy tavern not far from the lunar emptiness of the Alexanderplatz, and drank vodka, of course.

Freedom is the most important thing in the world, nodded the journalist in agreement, and bought Szív another glass of vodka.

The next day Szív received a letter from his wife. Pink envelope, with her familiar tiny letters slanting to the right. Mrs. Szív wrote her husband, among other things, that the word their son Lacika heard most often was

"Don't":

Don't do that, Lacika.

Not that either, Lacika.

Stop it, Lacika.

Finish it, Lacika, that's a good boy.

It's rather remarkable, wrote Mrs. Szív, that after so many refusals and denials one still grows up. Szív had to smile, for he thought just then: Why of course. Why else would one grow up but to be able to repeat, again and again:

Don't do that, son.

Not that either, my dear girl.

He thought of this as he opened the door of a small wine bar in Pankow on a brilliant autumn day, just before noon. There was a morning-after feeling in the air, drifting overhead like a stray, lost veil. It seemed as if everything about to pass was streaming forth, still resplendent.

The tavern, just around the corner from the park, was called the Parkklause, and while Szív was in Berlin it became part of his routine to stop in once a day. The place consisted of three separate but interconnecting areas; there was a small bar, with standing room only, then, off to the side, a stuffy, usually smelly dining room, and in the back, a billiard room. A dim hallway led to the toilet. It was here that Szív tasted apple liqueur for the first time in his life.

Freedom is the most important thing, Szív thought, as he was about to order his usual: a shot of vodka and a glass of beer. It was a fairly modest and reasonable combination. But the likable black-haired bartender had already placed the drinks on the counter. Well, well. Szív felt warm inside, and he broke into a smile. Here he was, wandering about in a strange city turned upside down by construction, and yet after only a few days there was someone who remembered him, who had come to know him a little. Szív tossed off the vodka and quickly gulped down the beer, so that he could ask for another round, out of gratitude. But then he changed his mind. He shuddered, got goose bumps—he hadn't enjoyed that vodka at all, and the beer was even worse. Flustered, he said good-bye and walked out clearing his throat, like someone who had been publicly humiliated.

Then he forgot the whole thing. He worked hard that day, writing a great deal, and was pleased with the results. Several pages of wonderful sentences, countless good thoughts, and plenty of ideas still waiting to be expanded.

After such a day one deserved a pleasant evening stroll on the Grabbenallee and a chance to stop in at the Parkklause again for a drink that would warm the heart. It was late, and wisdom prevailed in the tavern, the kind that comes just before closing time. Only a few slow-moving drunks stumbled about the bar, arguing in the downy, blue-gray cigarette smoke—*ja, nein, doch, vielleicht, na ja, wahrscheinlich, aber!* Behind the counter the black-haired bartender, whose features were more Slavic than German, greeted Szív with a smile and served him a shot of vodka and a beer. He nimbly slipped a round piece of paper on top of the beer glass to preserve the foam. Szív stared at the whole display and felt a coldness in his heart. He looked once more into the man's open, friendly face and sensed danger, an imminent surprise attack. Or, to put it another way, he stood at the edge of a precipice and felt that he was about to take the plunge. And this wasn't all; he wasn't the only one in peril. The others were, too, these local upholders of world order—Herr Jürgen, for example, who drank only Jägermeister; Hansi, the pensioner, who preferred ale; young Wilhelm, who always ordered a double vodka; and Auntie Gretchen, who drank apple liqueur. Caught together in the breezes of the October night, this assortment of East Germans, who seemed familiar because they were drunk, was also in danger. For as soon as they walked into the Parkklause, this likable barman nodded to them, and without further ado poured the Jägermeister, the ale, the double vodka, the apple liqueur—always the same for each customer. But this gesture, Szív realized, this appealing gesture, had to come from the Devil himself. For if freedom were the most important thing in the world, then the Devil's aim was to deprive you of your freedom; and he did this by binding, no, chaining you to cruel and stupid habits—habits that forced ignorance on your soul, reducing you to an animal state. Returning the bartender's still intact smile with one of his own, Szív sighed and said very quietly: "Excuse me, sir, but I think I'll have a glass of ale this time." The man's face turned rum red, then liqueur yellow; his eyebrows began to twitch, although he was quick to put his friendliest smile back on his face. Within seconds Szív was given his ale, which tasted so good he had to order another.

The next day Szív stopped at the Parkklause after visiting a few shops. The black-haired young man smiled at him, he may even have flashed his white teeth, but Szív felt there was something strange and ominous in the smile. He stared at the vodka and the beer that were already set before him and took a deep breath; then, wrinkling his forehead, he said that today he'd rather have a large brandy, and pointed toward the bottle.

A brandy, the man repeated.

A large one, whispered Szív, as though it hurt him to say it. The smile wilted on the bartender's friendly face. With a stern look he took the bottle off the glass shelf, poured the glass of brandy, and all but shoved it in Szív's face. Szív drank it, coughed a little, and then left, feeling the hostile stare of the other customers on his back. A nasty northerly whipped the tattered gray clouds in the sky, but Szív found himself humming cheerfully. A Honecker look-alike—such people were still to be seen in Berlin at this time—stared contemptuously at him from a street corner; Szív whistled and waved. Pimply schoolboys were smoking cigarettes at a bus stop. He mistook a bicycle lane for the sidewalk and was almost knocked over; the cyclist yelled at him furiously, but just for the hell of it, he smiled back. The world is what it is. German brandy is for the birds . . . God, it's awful. In his room he listened to Bach and read something by Ivo Andrić. Then he switched from baroque harpsichord to Annie Lennox, and wrote a few light and feathery sentences. He blew them gently around the room, and they fluttered about like tiny free spirits in heaven.

One such day Szív heard a very nice story about the Stasi, the former East German secret police. This particular story began when the Stasi got a woman—let's call her Corin—to work for them. Her job was to report on a man whom we shall call Hansi. They both worked in a state planning agency. There was nothing unusual about any of this, the number of East German women who spied on unsuspecting men in those years must have run in the millions. Corin diligently prepared her reports on Hansi. For months, years, like a dependable columnist, she submitted her few pages of text. She wrote even if she had a headache or a cold, or felt depressed, or if the full moon grinned at her from the sky. But once, while writing up one of her routine reports—she was describing what Hansi had said about Georg Lukács, the world-renowned Hungarian philosopher—Corin began to tremble, and the pen fell out of her hand. At the time she was living on the Grabbenallee, in a small studio apartment on the fourth floor. She staggered to the window, and stared through the curtain at the desolate nighttime scene below. Slowly she realized that she was done for, she'd fallen in love with this man. She loved the way he moved, his smell, the way he looked at her with arched eyebrows, and the way she sometimes looked back at him, her head tilted sideways. She thought that she would die if she ever had to stop writing about him. So she returned to her desk and finished her report, struggling to find smoother, subtler, more polished sentences than ever before. She did not use the flat, punctilious Prussian style, but wrote the way a Spaniard or a Turk might when denouncing a neighbor or enemy—with ardor, embellishing her sentences, letting passion ignite her soul. That night, while lying in bed, Corin thought about seeing him the next day in the office. How different it would be. She trembled again and let her fingers slide between her thighs. Miracles occurred even in East Germany!

The next day Hansi gave her an unexpected though unmistakable smile, and invited her to a little tavern in Kreuzberg. Afterward they made love as naturally as if they had been doing it for years and still couldn't get their fill of each other's body. Fluids, blood, emanations—everything blended together. Corin had at least four orgasms, and after the second she was sure that she had fainted for a few seconds. After dating for three months, they got married and were as happy as spring over the Jüteborg barracks. In the summer they traveled to Hungary, to the Plattensee, ate goulash and joked with the herdsmen on the plains. In Prague, in Wenceslas Square, they argued lightheartedly with the locals about which beer was better: Pilsner Urquell or Wernesgrüner. Once they even flew to Havana, where Corin happily threw up from too much Cuban rum, and a somewhat tipsy Hansi declared, while playing with rings of cigar smoke, that Fidel ought to try life without a beard. Eventually Corin became pregnant and bore Hansi a beautiful little girl. And all this time she continued to write reports about the man who was now her husband. She told the Stasi what Hansi thought about the Soviet presence in Afghanistan, about lax conditions in Hungary, and also how he felt about Ceaușescu, the Arab terrorists, God, death, and their neighbor Jakob Keller, who kept cats in his flat so the staircase reeked of them all the time. But we know how these things are. Some of the phrases Corin attributed to Hansi in her reports were hers, as were many of the opinions she recorded. Yes, without realizing what was happening, Corin managed to work into her reports the harmonious happiness of their family life.

When the moment of freedom arrived and the world eagerly carried off bits and pieces of the Wall, the government wisely—in fact, very wisely—opened the doors to the Stasi archives. Anyone who wanted to could walk into the former headquarters and read everything reported about them during those unhappy, restricted years. Hansi, too, wanted to know the truth. So one windy spring morning, having taken the day off from work, he kissed his wife—who hadn't, curiously, been well—on the forehead, and left, without telling her that instead of going off to work he was going to the Stasi archives to see his files. Expressionless and unblinking, he sat there from ten in the morning till four in the afternoon, reading the things that an agent named "Comrade Love"—that is, his wife, Corin—had written about him for twenty long years.

Szív thought about this story, more precisely about the moment when Hansi lifted his face, sighed, looked over the stacks of documents, and said: The most important thing in the world is freedom.

Szív walked into the Parkklause.

As always, the place smelled awful. Szív couldn't account for the particularly pungent smell, especially since on this early Sunday afternoon only a handful of people—bright-faced East German couples and ancient pensioners with trembling hands—were sitting around the cloth-covered tables in the dining room, and there weren't many customers in the bar. He shrugged his shoulders. And as he turned his head he encountered the openly hostile gaze of the bartender. He thought he saw hatred smoldering in that stare, and it terrified him. But it wasn't the man's narrow eyes, or his tightly pressed, bloodless lips, or his hateful demeanor that was so terrible, but the sudden thought that he would love to have a shot of vodka right now, with a glass of beer to chase it.

Heaven help me, just a small vodka, a small beer.

Unspeakable anger registered in the eyes of the decidedly unsympathetic bartender. He silently measured out the vodka, poured the beer, and with an abrupt motion pushed the foam-saver over the glass. Then he looked at Szív with a triumphant grin on his face. Szív felt that it was all over. He silently shook his head, yes, yes, and his hand slowly reached for the glass of vodka. His index finger was only a few inches away—Michelangelo's famous fresco may come to mind, where God and man almost touch—when Szív came to his senses. To hell with the touch. He knew that if he yielded to the other man's will here and now, he was lost. Then Ernő Szív would no longer be Ernő Szív, but a fake, a puppet, a stooge. Mustering all his strength, he pulled his hand back, smiled innocently, and asked for a glass of apple liqueur. It was an unexpected move, a stroke of genius. Apple liqueur instead of vodka and beer! The bartender seemed shaken, and a look of foolish bewilderment spread over his face. He pursed his lips, flared his nostrils, and stared for a moment into space. Then he shook his head.

"I didn't quite catch that," he said.

"I would like a glass of *Apfelkorn*, please," Szív said calmly, and indicated with his hand that he wanted a large one.

The next day he couldn't get out of bed. All morning he tossed and turned, retching whenever he thought of vodka and beer. He may have been feverish; in any case he sweated profusely, and every now and then cried out in pain. But if someone had told him that maybe he should not have had those five — perhaps six—large glasses of apple liqueur, that person would have been wrong: it was not a hangover that ailed him. No, yesterday he had fought for freedom, and it was this grueling struggle that had worn him out. Had the skeptics seen the wide-eyed, shocked look in the barman's eyes after the second glass, the sparks of anger after the third, the signs of total annihilation after the fourth; had they heard his insane laughter as he handed Szív the fifth glass, they would have agreed that this was an awesome struggle, a decisive, manly bout, the kind that must end in disaster for one of the combatants. But perhaps this enormous test of strength hadn't been resolved, perhaps it had only been interrupted. After all, victory must be seen, not just felt; you have to see your defeated foe's humiliation, his servile smile. After five—or perhaps six—liqueurs, however, it's hard to see anything. Szív, who had stumbled home with his heart soaked in apple liqueur, was afraid that he hadn't won after all. He knew that he'd visit the Parkklause again—what choice did he have?—but he also knew that he wouldn't have the strength to do anything but accept a vodka with a glass of beer if it were presented to him.

By the afternoon he had pulled himself together.

What now? Good Lord, what now?

The sky is above, the ground below, and man is suspended in between. Where is freedom?

He opened the door of the Parkklause, and in the billowing cigarette smoke of the afternoon crowd he spotted the dark, likable face of the bartender. It was a humble face, with the sad look of the vanquished. Szív came closer, still uncertain that he could pull it off. He waited and said nothing until the bartender lowered his eyes, perhaps even his head, too, and quietly asked: "What will you have, sir?" Szív didn't smile—he hated arrogant, complacent winners—but gave the bartender an earnest look and asked for a shot of vodka with a glass of beer. And this he received. The only thing to add to this story about a struggle for freedom is that for a good month, for the remainder of Szív's stay in Berlin, he never drank anything but vodka with beer at the Parkklause.

Translated from the Hungarian by Ivan Sanders

DURS GRÜNBEIN

Berlin Round

for Christian Döring

I *(Tauentzienstrasse)*

Here no more little songs go skipping down the street,
And the breeze, blowing by, cuts itself on the edges
Of glass and steel emporia, four stories high and stuffed with goods.
Those who live here do so hurriedly and at their peril.

At night, street sweeping machines produce the requisite sheerness of surface.
Above the sheen of ice-skating rinks, neon signs spread—
Rumorlike the names the phone book is crawling with.
The last bourgeois dramas pop up in the mid-season sales.

There's a church here, somewhat reminiscent of a bunker,
Since its snapped-off tower, a broken bottleneck, has been plugged
With the same stuff as provides the echoes in multistory parking garages.
If a smile emerges from the subway, it will encounter something Mannerist.

If there are teeth in the asphalt, they will be those of dispatch riders
Taking a tumble, or window cleaners plunged from their scaffolding.
The green traffic island serves as a trampoline. In the rush hour traffic,
Some spy fortune's wheel, while others merely cop a fine.

However much junk you cram in your pockets to take with you
When you go, enough will still remain in situ for the young lady archaeologist,
Kneeling in the ruins of fabled cities, in her hand a camel hair brush—
Distant, degenerate descendent of the mason's trowel.

II (*Anhalter Bahnhof*)

This is where the tanks about-turned
And papyrossa or peace pipe smoke fumed from their stumpy turrets.
No longer end of the line for any Reichsbahn train,
The Mongol hordes here hit the buffer.
Hellas-Express. The departure of the rich and beautiful,
Cushioned in their private compartments, for the warm south.
A Russian stood as pointsman
Collecting watches, jewelry, the victor's tithe.
The level crossings were marked in Cyrillic. Charred roof beams
Pointed the way through avenues of ruins.
To smirk at the red star would have been
The gravest sacrilege. They let it go, the idea
Of razing Berlin, that nest of vipers, like Carthage,
Leaving the shadow of a metropolis in the Brandenburg sand.
Then goulash steamed and Cossacks danced,
Even if old mother Krause had nothing to laugh about.

III (Friedrichshain)

No, that was no welcome—
Look at the bullet holes in home after home.
Those were volleys, not salvos,
Back then in Friedrichshain.

There wasn't much fraternization.
Anyone in a machine-gun emplacement fired for what he was worth
Maybe the dogs and the shrubs in the park
Picked up a trick or two.

The white flags were taken down by a cold winter.
Sheets and bandages were needed.
That pleas went unheeded in the cellars
Is something you can sense in Friedrichshain.

IV *(Potsdamer Platz)*

They're churning up the ground for the capital city *in spe*.
Earth removers go in in advance of the nocturnal desolation.
Germania in her bunker, stretched out on her Prussian chaise longue,
Is disturbed in her sleep, and rolls over in the dirt.

It takes *Downtown Berlin* to help the diva loosen up.
Then, panting for it, the great Valkyrie spreads her thighs.
The brain, in its lucid moments of bitterness,
Sniffs something that cries out for destruction.

V (Epilogue)

What's going on here, you ask, nothing looks familiar
As you hunch under cranes. Didn't you use to be a giant
And have the place at your feet? Squares shrank to Liliputian scale
When you surfaced. One "Atchoo" brought down whole apartment blocks.

This used to be waste ground, sand and a bit of scorched grass,
Not marked on the map. Now no one believes you when you say
Goya's colossus used to sit here, waiting for it to revert to steppe.
You dropped your guard, and everything was suddenly knocked down.

The Prussian blue afternoon—four sectors, two variants—
Has turned into an hour of gray exhaust, as Tom, Dick and Harry
Crawl past each other in the rush. Half the population
Is stuck in traffic, their watchword "Faster living!"

Show the ancients the score. Not much sign of the Graces
But lockstep and tunnel vision aplenty. Who needs a key for the door,
The way prefab apartments squelch out of cement mixers?
One day your eye lights on reptiles battened to the glass facades

Unblinking, impassive—supervising the evictions.
It's only habit, downsized, that keeps returning to its dead haunts.

Translated from the German by Michael Hofmann

ARES ÖREN

Mrs. Kutzer's Neighbors

One day, a crazed wind
whisked away a Turk's mustache
and chasing after his mustache, the Turk
found himself on Naunyn Street.

He was a silent, innocuous,
middle-aged man.
He'd settled into Mrs. Kutzer's bottom floor.
Thinking of nothing else, he saved his money.
Then, one fine day, just as he'd come,
he silently left.
He left, yet,
in his wake
women and men,
their spouses and children,
his fellow countrymen swarmed in . . .
And a fresh, hate-filled,
longing-filled, hope-filled
steppe air engulfed
Naunyn Street.
And Naunyn Street put

those lost people
from wild lands
to sleep
on her dark damp breast.
As countless nights and mornings
passed
everyone on that street,
everything on that street,
became an accepted part of one another.
So much so that
a Naunyn Street without Turks today
might not want for streetness, yet
at the end of its elderly days
it would be denied a childlike beginning.

Lullaby for Türkiye

We're such handsome men with our twirled mustaches
Men who live two worlds in one life
Men who are awake in dreams and dreaming while awake

How cunning that wooden horse is, ah, the enemy within
It constantly neighs in a deep corner of our hearts
Saz lutes play and we dance in the bosom of the sad night

Translated from the Turkish by Erdağ M. Göknar

1

HANNAH HÖCH

In 1939, Hannah Höch, seeking a state of "inner emigration," moved from Berlin's centrally located Friedenau neighborhood to the suburb of Heiligensee, where nobody would be aware, as she put it, of her "lurid past as a Dadaist or cultural Bolshevist." Many of Höch's male colleagues from her Dada years and after — such as the activist John Heartfield and Höch's close friend Kurt Schwitters — had been forced into exile during the rise of the Nazis. As a female artist, Höch was less conspicuous, but she was in danger not only as a former Dadaist but also due to her lesbian relationship with the Dutch avant-garde poet Til Brugman. Nevertheless, Höch stayed in Germany and even illustrated a book of Brugman's, *Scheingehacktes (Mock Mincemeat)*, in 1935, which contained a veiled parody of the National Socialists. Her art sales dried up because venues were closed to her (in 1932 her one-woman show planned for the Dessau Bauhaus was canceled when the Nazis abolished the school).

During the Third Reich, Höch's personal life was in upheaval as well. In 1935 she ended her nine-year relationship with Brugman and began a love affair with Kurt Matthies, a man twenty-one years her junior. They married in 1938, when Höch was forty-eight. But three years after they had settled in Heiligensee, Matthies left her abruptly. From 1942 to 1945, with almost all her friends in exile, money in short supply, and a low profile essential, Höch found herself alone for long periods of time. Throughout these years, she persevered to an astonishing degree in her art, producing watercolors, gouaches, paintings, and photomontages. She expressed her revulsion toward both the Nazi regime and World War II through works such as her *Totentanz (Dance of the dead)* gouache series of 1943.

After the war, the hot, highly saturated colors of illustrated magazines like *Life International* provided Höch with material for her photomontages, in which she created luscious abstractions in reaction to the realism promoted by the National Socialists. But by the 1960s Höch had returned to exploring images of women, a theme that had been important to her in the 1920s. In *Fremde Schönheit II (Strange Beauty II)*, 1966, an elegantly clothed European body is topped by an ethnographic head. The head looks like a protective mask, as much a costume as the evening gown the figure is wearing. The work calls into question archetypal standards of beauty.

Also exploring the theme of female masquerade, but more playful and cutting, is Höch's *Entartet (Degenerate)*, from 1969. In it, a slinky, silvery female torso with pointed, red-tipped breasts poses in profile on a shimmering, translucent background surrounded by decorative dragonflies. The title of the work, *Entartet*, is a double entendre. "Degenerate" was the word the Nazis used to condemn modern art, most famously in the *Entartete Kunst* exhibition, which opened in Munich in July 1937, and moved to Berlin later that year. But the Nazis also used this word in reference to alternative sexualities, as well as to nonreproductive hetero-sexuality. Höch's *Entartet* is joyfully defiant and erotic, even while it toys with the idea of seduction as weapon. Its forms shine and buzz, after all, even as they threaten.

Höch remained highly creative and productive in all the decades of her adult life; *Entartet* was created when she was eighty years old. In fact, it was not until the 1970s — when Höch was in her eighties — that she enjoyed an international revival through major museum retrospectives. In a photomontage of this time, she portrayed herself — sharp-eyed, white-haired, intently smiling — surrounded by her work.

Maud Lavin

Das Fest kann beginnen (On with the Party), 1965.
Institut für Auslandsbeziehungen, Stuttgart.

LEFT:
Fremde Schönheit II (Strange Beauty II), 1966.
Institut für Auslandsbeziehungen, Stuttgart.

RIGHT:
Entartet (Degenerate), 1969.
Landesbank, Berlin.

PAGE 28:
Magie (Magic), 1966.
Berlinische Galerie, Landesmuseum für Moderne
Kunst, Photographie und Architektur, Berlin.

Little Queen of the Lovely Whores
to Juan Carlos Onetti

I.
Advent stars are blinking
in the windows of the El Dorado.
She keeps her stockings on, I
my shirt. We do it to me, her,
us. While leaving
I see the marks
left by stiletto heels
in the door's wood, knee-high.
It's night. It's raining.
Snails are breathing
on the embassy walls
in Tiergarten. Somebody
is howling about unity
and money.

II.
I'm going to Venezuela,
she said (with those long,
suggestive steps), and my
camera is broken. There is no
fixing the remembered
nation, I said,
put your
picture candle in your eye.
So we got ourselves a tan,
the best we could
in the late winter. But nobody,
she says, will rob me
of my night.

III.
In the theater of the sensitive,
there was love for a moment of unrest.
Then the quickening hour
of the heedless Saturday headed
toward evening.
Flashback: I look at
you. You keep yourself shut.
Adieu, see you soon. Always,
fear is the trick
of voyeurs.

Translated from the German by Andrew Shields

GÜNTER KUNERT

Mid-July

Even early in the day
such oppressive heat. Along
the street drawn curtains.
Shade: circumscribed and fleeting.
Plodding paces once in a while.
Later a front door gently
falls shut. If only
darkness were already here
night birds from the plain
from all the corners of the earth
rising above us: with ever faster
wing beats of their hours
flying off unchained
at the break of dawn.

Berlin, paleontologically

Here all the sediments are exposed:
history laid out in layers—
blood, sweat, and filth, permeated with hope,
that leads through the strata of bygone eras.

The city: fossil on every side—
deceased time locked within itself.
You dare not avert your eyes
so they remain: as the present.

Translated from the German by Peter Constantine

A VISIT TO THE PERGAMON ALTAR

PETER WEISS

ALL AROUND US THE BODIES rose out of the stone, crowded into groups, intertwined, or shattered into fragments, hinting at their shapes with a torso, a propped-up arm, a burst hip, a scabbed shard, always in warlike postures, dodging, rebounding, attacking, shielding themselves, stretched high or crooked, some of them snuffed out, but with a freestanding, forward-pressing foot, a twisted back, the contour of a calf harnessed into a single common motion. A gigantic struggle, emerging from the gray wall, recalling perfection, sinking back into formlessness. A hand, stretching upward from the rough ground, ready to clutch, attached to the shoulder across empty surface, a mangled face, with yawning cracks, a wide-open mouth, blankly gaping eyes, the face surrounded by the flowing locks of the beard, the tempestuous folds of a garment, everything close to its weathered end and close to its origin. Every detail preserving its expression, brittle fragments from which the whole could be gleaned, rough stumps next to polished smoothness, enlivened by the play of muscles and sinews, tautly harnessed chargers, rounded shields, erect spears, a head split into a raw oval, outspread wings, a triumphantly raised arm, a leaping heel encircled by a fluttering tunic, a clenched fist on a now absent sword, shaggy hounds, their jaws clamped into loins and necks, a falling man, his finger stub aiming at the eye of the beast hanging over him, a charging lion protecting a female warrior, his paw swinging back to strike, hands endowed with bird claws, horns looming from weighty brows, scaly legs coiling, serpents everywhere, with strangleholds around bellies and throats, darting their tongues, baring sharp teeth, bashing into naked chests. These just created, already dying faces, these tremendous and dismembered hands, these wide-sweeping

34

pinions drowning in the blunt rock, this stony gaze, these lips torn open to·
shriek, this striding, stamping, these blows of heavy weapons, this rolling of
armored wheels, these clusters of hurled lightning bolts, this grinding
underfoot, this rearing and collapsing, this endless straining to twist upward
out of grainy boulders. And how gracefully curly the hair, how elaborately
gathered and girded the lightweight mantle, how delicate the ornamentation
on the straps of the shield, on the bulge of the helmet, how gentle the
shimmer of the skin, ready for caresses yet exposed to the relentless rivalry,
to slaughter and annihilation. With masklike countenances, clutching one
another and shoving one another away, strangling one another, clambering
over one another, sliding from horses, entangled in the reins, utterly
vulnerable in their nakedness, and yet enrapt in Olympic aloofness,
appearing indomitable as an ocean monster, a griffin, a centaur, yet
grimacing in pain and despair; thus they clashed with one another, acting at
higher behest, dreaming, motionless in insane vehemence, mute in an
inaudible roaring, all of them woven into a metamorphosis of torture,
shuddering, persisting, waiting for an awakening, in perpetual endurance
and perpetual rebellion, in outrageous impact, and in an extreme exertion to
subdue the threat, to provoke the decision. A soft ringing and murmuring
resounded now and again, the echoes of footfalls and voices surrounded us
for moments at a time, and then, once more, only this battle was near, our
gazes glided over toes in their sandals, bouncing off the skull of a fallen man,
over the dying man whose stiffening hand lay tenderly on the arm of the
goddess who held him by the hair. The cornice was the ground for the
warriors, from its narrow, even strip they threw themselves up into the
turmoil, the hooves of the horses banged upon the cornice, the hems of the
garments grazed it, and the serpentine legs twisted across it. The ground was
breached at only one place: here, the demoness of the earth rose up, her face
hacked away under her eye sockets, her breasts massive beneath a thin
serape, the torn-off clump of one hand lifted in a search, the other hand,
asking for a standstill, loomed from the stone edge, and long, knotty fingers
stretched up to the profiled corbel, as if they were still underground and were
trying to reach the wrist of the open thumbless female hand; they moved
along under the cornice, seeking the blurred traces of incised script, and
Coppi's face, his myopic eyes behind glasses with a thin steel frame,

examined the letters, which Heilmann deciphered with the help of a book he
had brought along. Coppi turned toward him, attentive, with a broad,
sharply drawn mouth, a large, protruding nose, and we gave the opponents
in this melee their names and, in the torrent of noise, discussed the causes of
the struggle. Heilmann—the fifteen-year-old, who rejected any uncertainty,
who tolerated no undocumented interpretation but occasionally also
adhered to the poetic demand for a conscious deregulation of the senses,
who wanted to be a scientist and a seer, he, whom we nicknamed our
Rimbaud, explained to us, who were already about twenty years old and who
had been out of school for four years by now and were familiar with the world
of labor and also with unemployment, while Coppi had spent a year in prison
for circulating subversive literature—Heilmann explained to us the meaning
of this round dance, in which the entire host of deities, led by Zeus, was
striding toward victory over a race of giants and fabulous creatures. The
Titans, the sons of the lamenting Gaea, in front of whose torso we were now
standing, had blasphemously mutinied against the gods; but other struggles
that had passed across the kingdom of Pergamum were concealed under this
depiction. The regents in the dynasty of the attalids had ordered their master
sculptors to translate the swift transience, paid for with thousands of lives, to
a level of timeless permanence, thereby putting up a monument to their own
grandeur and immortality. The subjugation of the Gallic tribes invading from
the north had turned into a triumph of aristocratic purity over wild and base
forces, and the chisels and mallets of the stonecarvers and their assistants
had displayed a picture of incontestable order to make the subjects bow in
awe. Historic events appeared in mythical disguise, enormously palpable,
arousing terror, admiration, not understandable as man-made, but
endurable only as a more-than-personal power that wanted hordes of
enthralled, enslaved people, though there were few at the top who dictated
destinies with a mere stirring of the finger. The populace, when trudging by
on solemn days, scarcely dared to glance up at the effigy of its own history,
while along with the priests, the philosophers and poets, the artists from
elsewhere, all full of factual knowledge, had long since walked around the
temple; and that which lay in magical darkness for the ignorant was, for the
informed, a handicraft to be soberly assessed. The initiates, the specialists
talked about art, praising the harmony of movement, the coordination of

gestures; the others, however, who were not even familiar with the concept of culture, stared furtively into the figures' gaping maws, felt the swoop of the paw in their own flesh. The work gave pleasure to the privileged; the others sensed a segregation under a draconian law of hierarchy. However, a few sculptures, said Heilmann, did not have to be extracted from their symbolism; the falling man, the man of Gaul taking his own life, showed the immediate tragedy of a concrete situation. But these sculptures, replied Coppi, had not been outside, they had remained among the trophies in the throne rooms, purely to indicate from whom the shields and helmets, the swords and spears had been taken. The sole aim of the wars was to safeguard the territories of the kings. The gods, confronted with the spirits of the earth, kept the notion of certain power relationships alive. A frieze filled with anonymous soldiers, who, as tools of the higher-ups, fought for years, attacking other anonymous soldiers, would have altered the attitude of those they served toward them, boosting their position; the kings, not the warriors, won the victories, and the victors could be like the gods, while the losers were despised by the gods. The privileged knew that the gods did not exist, for they who donned the masks of the gods knew themselves. So they were even more insistent on being surrounded with splendor and dignity. Art served to lend their rank, their authority, the appearance of the supernatural. They could permit no skepticism about their perfection. Heilmann's bright face, with its regular features, bushy eyebrows, and high forehead, had turned to the demoness of the Earth. She had brought forth Uranos, the sky, Pontos, the sea, and all mountains. She had given birth to the giants, the Titans, the Cyclops, and the Furies. This was our race. We evaluated the history of the earthly beings. We looked up at her again, the demoness stretching out of the ground. Waves of loosened hair flowed around her. On her shoulder, she carried a bowl of pomegranates. Foliage and grape vines twirled at the back of her neck. The start of the lips, begging for mercy, was discernible in the raw facial plane, which veered sideways and upward. A gash gaped from her chin to her larynx. Alkyoneus, her favorite son, leaned away from her while dropping to his knees. The stump of his left hand groped toward her. She was still touching his left foot, which dangled from his stretched and shattered leg. His thighs, abdomen, belly, and chest were all tensed in convulsions. The pain of death radiated from the small wound inflicted

37

between his ribs by the venomous reptile. The wide, unfurled wings of the
kingfisher, growing from his shoulder, slowed his plunge. The silhouette of
the burst-off face above him, with the hard line of the neck, of the hair tied up
and tucked under the helmet, spoke of the pitilessness of Athena. As she
swung forward, her wide, belted cloak flew back. The downward glide of her
garment revealed, on her left breast, the scale armor bearing the small,
bloated face of Medusa. The weight of the round shield, her arm thrust into
its thong, pulled her along to new deeds. Nike, leaping up, with mighty
wings, in a loose, airy tunic, held a wreath, invisible but implied by the
gesture, over her head. Heilmann pointed at the dissolving goddess of the
night, Nyx, who, with a loving smile, was hurling her vessel full of serpents
toward a downcast creature; at Zeus, who, in his open, billowing cloak, was
using his woolen aegis, the goatskin of doom, to whip three adversaries; and
at Eos, the goddess of dawn, who was riding like a cloud in front of the rising
team of the naked sun god Helios. Thus, he said gently, a new day dawns
after the dreadful butchery, and now the glass-covered room became noisy
with the scraping of feet on the smooth floor, with the ticking echoes of shoe
soles on the steep steps leading up the reconstructed western facade of the
temple, to the colonnades of the interior court. We turned back toward the
relief, which throughout its scenes demonstrated the instant when the
tremendous change was about to take place, the moment when the
concentrated strength portends the ineluctable consequence. By seeing the
lance immediately before its throw, the club before its whizzing plunge, the
run before the jump, the hauling-back before the clash, our eyes were driven
from figure to figure, from one situation to the next, and the stone began to
quiver all around us. However, we missed Heracles, who, according to the
myth, was the only mortal to ally himself with the gods in the battle against
the giants; and, combing the immured bodies, the remnants of limbs, we
looked for the son of Zeus and Alkmene, the earthly helper whose courage
and unremitting labor would bring an end to the period of menace. All we
could make out was a sign bearing his name, and the paw of a lion's skin that
had cloaked him; nothing else testified to his station between Hera's four-
horse team and Zeus's athletic body; and Coppi called it an omen that
Heracles, who was our equal, was missing, and that we now had to create our
own image of this advocate of action. As we headed toward the low, narrow

exit on the side of the room, the red armbands of the men in black and brown
uniforms shone toward us from the whirling shifts in the throng of visitors;
and whenever I spotted the emblem, rotating and chopping in the white,
round field, it became a venomous spider, ruggedly hairy, hatched in with
pencil, ink, or india ink, in Coppi's hand, as I knew it from the class at the
Scharfenberg Institute, where Coppi had sat at the next desk, doodling on
small pictures, cards from cigarette packs, on illustrations clipped from
newspapers, disfiguring the symbol of the new rulers, adding warts, tusks,
nasty creases, and rivulets of blood to the plump faces looming from the
uniform collars. Heilmann, our friend, also wore the brown shirt with rolled-
up sleeves, the shoulder straps, the string for the whistle, the dagger on the
short pants; but he wore this garb as a disguise to camouflage his own
knowledge and to camouflage Coppi, who was coming from illegal work, and
to camouflage me, who was about to leave for Spain. And thus, on September
22, 1937, a few days before my departure, we stood in front of the altar frieze,
which had been brought here from the castle mountain of Pergamum to be
reconstructed, and which, painted in colors and lined with forged metals, had
once reflected the light of the Aegean sky. . . . We looked back at a prehistoric
past, and for an instant the prospect of the future likewise filled up with a
massacre impenetrable to the thought of liberation. Heracles would have to
help them, the subjugated, and not those who had enough armor and
weapons. Prior to the genesis of the figurations, there had been the bondage,
the enclosure in stone. In the marble quarries on the mountain slopes north of
the castle, the master sculptors had pointed their long sticks at the best blocks
while eyeing the Gaulic captives toiling in the sultry heat. Shielded and fanned
by palm branches, squinting in the blinding sun, the sculptors took in the
rippling of the muscles, the bending and stretching of the sweating bodies.
The defeated warriors, driven here in chains, hanging from ropes on the rock
faces, smashing crowbars and wedges into the strata of glittering, bluish
white, crystalline limestone, and transporting the gigantic ashlars on long
wooden sleds down the twisting paths, were notorious for their savagery, their
brutal customs, and in the evenings the lords with their retinues passed them
timidly when the stinking prisoners, drunk on cheap rotgut, were camping in
a pit. Up in the gardens of the castle, however, in the gentle breeze wafting up
from the sea, the huge bearded faces became the stuff of the sculptors'

dreams, and they remembered ordering one man or another to stand still, opening his eyes wide, pulling his lips apart to view his teeth, they recalled the arteries swelling on his temples, the glistening nose, zygomata, and forehead emerging from the cast shadows. They could still hear the lugging and shoving, the stemming of shoulders and backs against the weight of the stone, the rhythmic shouts, the curses, the whip cracks, the grinding of sled runners in the sand, and they could see the figures of the frieze slumbering in the marble coffins. Slowly they chiseled forth the limbs, felt them, saw forms emerge whose essence was perfection. With the plundered people transferring their energies into slack and receptive thoughts, degradation and lust for power produced art. Through the noisy maelstrom of a school class we pushed our way into the next room, where the market gates of Miletus loomed in the penumbra. At the columns flanking the gates, which had led from the town hall of the port to the open emporium, Heilmann asked whether we had noticed that inside, in the altar room, space had been inverted, so that exterior surfaces had become interior walls. In facing the western perron, he said, we had our backs to the eastern side—the rear of the temple, that is, in its merely rudimentary reconstruction—and the unfolded southern frieze stretched out to the right while the relief on the northern cornice ran to the left.

Something the viewer was to grasp by slowly circling it was now surrounding him instead. This dizzying procedure would ultimately make us understand the theory of relativity, he added, when, moving a few centuries deeper, we walked along the clay brick walls that had once stood in the cluster of Nebuchadnezzar's Babylonian towers, and we then suddenly stepped into an area where yellowing leaves, whirring sunspots, pale yellow double-decker buses, cars with flashing reflections, streams of pedestrians, and the rhythmic smashing of hobnailed boots demanded a readjustment in our bearings, a new indication of our whereabouts.

Translated from the German by Joachim Neugroschel

VOLKER BRAUN

The Hill of the Dead

Caesar watched from his tumulus
The distant sea battle *Barbarian ships* the maker of history
Sweating with fear *After that it was a question*
Of sheer courage and billhooks
Ripping down the yards and the leather sails
BELLUM GALLICUM the usual Gulf War
Played out before the eyes of the land army on the cliff top cinema
And the sudden drop in the wind
And that's how empires are made / I've seen them fall
Perched on his bones the Führer's bunker
Grotewohlstrasse in the other Germany
The surprising onshore wind in the corridors
History blinks its eyes not to be blinded
Reeling THE DANCE ON THE WALL
The wall peckers with their little hammers
The *Volksarmee* looking on the army of the unemployed
One minute of my time

Following the Massacre of the Illusions

Guevara under the march route with severed
Hands, "no more burrowing for him,"
When ideas are buried
The bones emerge
A state funeral FOR FEAR OF RESURRECTION
The head marked with blood and wounds a design concept
FOR ONCE FOLLOW UP YOUR PHRASES
TO THE POINT WHERE THEY BECOME FLESH AND BLOOD
Valeri Chodemtchuk, interred
In the sarcophagus of the reactor to abide
However long the earth can take us
And what we will call freedom

The Bay of the Deceased

Demesne of the weather and the salt tides, the bay is the collection point for the deceased.
It swills them down from their failed runnels and vitas, their boats whose broken keels are
stranded on the bottom. Ever since human memory, they've been lying there, *little dunes of
bonemeal*, only reluctantly making room for the new arrivals that are tipped over them. They are
never really *buried*. They wait, while they still have their bones or their powers of thought, to be
ferried across to the isles of the blessed. That obsession grips all of us, as soon as we arrive
here. The blessed are those who are vindicated by life or death. I experienced that triumph
myself: when we who had failed were borne up again, long after our destruction, and *vindicated*
by history. As though intoxicated, we wallowed in the unhoped-for tide. The beaches peopled by
our merry millions! But wherever we appeared, we were met with bitterness and recrimination.
Vicious looks turned us away. What did we have to reproach ourselves for? What was our crime?
The fact that we had wanted to change the world, which was being swept away. Now sardonic
laughter answered us. We were the traitors who had given it false hope. Many of the dead shared
our fate—the history in which they had triumphed no longer existed. Now we were the scum.
A mad world: now we were to blame, we who had opposed its existence. Our laughter gurgled
in the swill. But salvation was at hand, they were building us a bridge to the islands. Just go,
they told us (everyone knows the voices), you and your hopes, just go. Admit it, you're dead and
betrayed. And that we certainly were. We took a deep breath. It's red and bloody, swear it off.
Bury this flag. *It will never be any different.* Then you will be among the blessed, leaving the stage
to applause. We listened to the words so easily said, and looked across to the islands. There we
would find peace. We could bury the whole matter. We heard ourselves laughing, and the bay
gurgled. The dead looked up with dead eyes and continued to hold their breath. Yes, we said,
it was a mistake. And we are already across. But it wasn't always a mistake, and not from the
outset.—What, you miserable ones, you don't want to be saved.—Not under that condition,
not at that price. So we said, and felt ourselves laughing still as we sank deeper, down to the lost
but not discouraged ones on the bottom. That I can attest to.

Translated from the German by Michael Hofmann

A SITE FOR CONTINGENCIES

INGEBORG BACHMANN

NOW AN AIRPLANE FLIES through the room every minute, brushing past the hook for the washcloth, its undercarriage a hand's breadth above the soap dish. Just before they land—their approach path goes through all the rooms— the planes must fly more quietly. The hospitals have complained. The planes have muted themselves, but it is more horrible than before. They hum above the heads, above the sweat-matted hair, these muted airplanes swooping by under the ceiling. In the hospitals there is an incredible uproar over all the planes, which cut their engines and become so quiet that you no longer hear them. But you listen anyway, from the moment you begin to hear a faint whine, as if you had a tuning fork at your ear; then you hear them better, then they are here, then they are gone, then there's a faintly perceptible drone, and then no more. Then the next not-quite-there sound begins, and again you are dissatisfied at being barely able to hear it; the doctor in charge has to go out to the street to check and show them his findings, to wave around all the sheets covered with hieroglyphics. This takes care of things for a moment, but in the next plane-free instant all the church bells in Berlin ring out, churches rise out of the ground, looming near—nothing but new, spartan, unadorned churches, with bell towers and Protestant tape recordings. The uproar over the clanging increases, where is the mayor, people scream that the churches should get out of here. The patients howl, take refuge in the corridor, water runs from the rooms into the corridor, mixed with blood because some of the patients have bitten their tongues on account of the churches. The hospital pastor sits in the visitor's chair, telling over and over how he studied to be a ship's pastor and has rounded the Cape of Good Hope. He knows nothing of bells. He takes a cracker from the plate, but no one dares say anything about the cracker and the bells, and he doesn't ask, either, whether anything is wrong, he just twirls his green hunter's hat in his hands. They ask him to leave, as the place must be aired out.

The corridors have to be mopped again already. Some well-known people have been brought in secretly, by ambulance at night, but most of them are relatives, none of them can provide any support. They have addresses, but no next of kin. Most important point: the next of kin. They all lie silent. The night nurse says he is on the way, he's coming from here or there, a plane is just arriving, it will happen, you can count on it. The next of kin must be what is meant. The doctor is expecting the plane any minute, he's pinned his hopes on it. Then, to calm things down, he says that next week everyone can go home. They all cough and hope, thermometers in their armpits, under their tongues, in their anuses, and needles some ten centimeters long in their flesh. The dark balconies are crumbling, tonight no one dares climb onto the railing to threaten the night nurse, who is making coffee again for the night doctor. They are all making plans alone. The plan is a tunnel, or you would have to go straight out into the desert, would have to free the camel from the zoo, untie it, saddle it up, ride on it through Brandenburg. You could depend on the camel. Then in the middle of the night there is a fee increase, and sweat breaks out like never before. It's perfectly dreadful. The room now costs a thousand goldmarks. They all grope for their call bells and press the button.

The disabled hobble down the steps of the Bellevue S-Bahn station, the light flickers as in a vault. Most are wearing armbands, yellow with black circles, with canes to support their ghostly, abbreviated limbs. Everything is disabled, not by bullets but internally. The bodies are muddled, they are too short above or below, the flesh on the faces is lifeless and paralyzed, the corners of mouths and eyes are crooked, and the fitful shadows of the train station make everything even worse. The woman behind the ticket window has to hold the ceiling as well as the S-Bahn up, for it's roaring again. Luckily the woman has gigantic muscles and hands. She supports the S-Bahn yet again as the train going to Friedrichstrasse rolls past overhead, at the same time as she hands out tickets. A piece of the ceiling falls down, but she lifts it up again, then another part collapses, the part on which the Victory Column stands, and a train clatters by again,

heading to Wannsee. It's a catastrophe. The people seek refuge in the adjoining restaurant, crouching under the tables, they want to wait out the attack, but the woman from the station comes and says it's no attack, service has returned to normal, it won't happen again.

The doctor must not be disturbed. The results have been determined for years, but won't be revealed. It must be a "disharmony." Something is seeping through the whole city; everyone is sure they have read or heard "disharmony," and some have even thought it, but publicly it's nowhere to be found. Still more trees are being planted, all in the sand, trees from the desert experience. The whole city finally goes to work, silently, everyone in fresh white shirts closed at the neck. There is no longer any uproar. Everything is muted. Most of them are half asleep.

Berlin has been tidied up. The stores have been put one on top of the other, layered in a pile, lying around its edges, clearly recognizable, are the shoes and rulers, rice and potato supplies, and coal, of course, all the coal that the City Senate has stored up. The sand is everywhere now—in the shoes, on the coal. The big display windows on top, the ones with the mysterious names Neckermann and Defeka, form a glass ceiling covering everything, you look through it but can't make out much. Below it, a pub is still open in Alt-Moabit, but no one understands how it's possible. After all, the city has been tidied up. The owner pours double schnapps, then buys a round himself; his pub was the best, the oldest, always full of people. But these people are no longer in Berlin. He buys another round, it's always drunk right up, then still another. And so it goes: double schnapps, large beer, always double. The

Spree and the Teltow Canal have already been filled up with schnapps, the Havel is foaming to the brim with beer, no one can speak clearly any longer beneath the many layers of glass, everything that's said runs out the corners of mouths, barely comprehensible. No one wants to talk anymore either, they speak only to say something, anything, and in any case everything runs out of the corners of their mouths and away, everything double.

Kreuzberg is on the way up now. Its damp cellars and old sofas are again in demand, the stovepipes, the rats, the view of the back courtyard. In addition you have to let your hair grow long, bum around, shout out; you have to preach, be drunk, and frighten old people, from the Hallesche Tor to the Böhmische Dorf. You have to always be alone and in a group, dragging some people along from one belief to the next. The new religion comes from Kreuzberg, the prophets' beards and the commands, the revolt against the subsidized agony. Everyone has to eat out of the same tin bowls, a very thin Berlin broth along with dark bread, and afterward one must order the sharpest schnapps, and then still more schnapps for the longest nights. The junk dealers aren't selling cheap anymore, since the area is on its way up. The Lantern to the World is making a go of it, the preachers and disciples let themselves be gawked at in the evening, and spit into the curried wurst of the curious. A century that does not want to reveal itself here either is called to account. The door of a house, any house, is rattled, a lamppost pushed over, and some passersby hit over the head. In Berlin it's OK to laugh.

After midnight all the bars are full. The Egg Shell, The Bath Tub, The Horse Stall, Kleist Kasino, Taboo, Chez Nous, Riverboat, Big Apple, and the Eden Saloon are all shaking with throbbing music, a shaking that breaks out in the night, always for a few hours only. The turnover increases, right away there is an inflation of damp hands and glazed eyes. At night all Berlin is a place for turnover and exchange. Everything gets mixed up in confusion, then some people pull away. Espionage has an easy time of it, every collapse is transparent. Everyone is out to get rid of his own secret, to surrender his news, to break down during interrogation. Everyone has everyone else on his neck, and in the dim light no one can check the bill foisted on them. Outside it's morning again, it's too bright. No more tabs are run. But no one knows about the transvestites, in what form and with what seal on their made-up lips they will go home and fall asleep, happily, into each day.

No one, least of all the new arrivals, believes that all the animals really live at the Zoo Station. No one is prepared for the camel. The Victory Column is now standing on his hump. The platforms empty very quickly on account of the animals, the men go to the aquarium, the women to the monkey house. The men stand for hours before the fishes, then before the tiny lizards. They have eyes for nothing but green-gold lizards, gentle, gentlest, that they would like to take with them, but the guards at the door pat down even breast pockets, there is nothing to be done. The women, all far apart from one another and suspicious of each other, visit their special monkeys. They have brought along silver spoons and silk bags, and offer sugar only to their own monkeys. Only just before closing time do the men and women meet, in the greenhouse on the bridge, above an indicated river. Below, crocodiles doze in the stuffy heat, everyone gazes down with eyes growing heavier and heavier, but the crocodiles don't put on a show, they just wait. The bridge could collapse now, bringing the crocodiles to life, but it doesn't collapse. No one can fall off unless deliberately pushed. The temperature can't rise, because it is precisely regulated, but it rises anyway. They all don't want to look at the crocodiles any longer, and push their way out, wanting to be home for their evening engagements.

—1964

Translated from the German by Burton Pike

REPORTAGE FROM WEIMAR BERLIN

JOSEPH ROTH

All around the Victory Column

The sky has donned its prettiest blue, as though planning a trip to the photographer's, and the March sun is distinctly philanthropic. The Victory Column rises into the air, slender and naked as a sunbather. In accordance with the rules governing popularity, it has recently acquired a prominence that only a failed terrorist attack is capable of producing.

For many years, it was fairly lonely. Street photographers with long-legged tripods used it as an inexpensive background for their grinning subjects. It was a knickknack left over from German history, something for foreign visitors to buy picture postcards of, or a suitable destination for an educational class outing. No German adult ever climbed up it.

But now, at noon, there are between two hundred and three hundred Berliners standing around the column, sniffing the lingering aroma of an unusual event, chewing the political fat.

I know for a fact that the gentleman in the cape and broad-brimmed hat who looks like a mushroom from the darkest depths of the Tiergarten is a secret scholar who deals with such things as the crystallization of quartz. Every day for the past quarter century, it has been his custom to pace up and down a nearby avenue, dependable as a brass pendulum weight, before returning home. But today, lo! He walked up his avenue, and then made straight for the Victory Column. And now he listens attentively to a short fellow discussing picric acid, waving his hat every now and then with one hand, wiping a blue-bordered handkerchief across his sweaty skull with the other.

I don't know whether picric acid has any particular bearing on the crystallization of quartz, but the quartz expert's interest in the stuff seems inexhaustible.

"Dynamite"—I overhear—"is dangerous. Dynamite is used to blast tunnels. It is even more dangerous when it's kept shut up in a cardboard box."

"What surprises me is that they didn't smell the burning fuse right away," observes a lady. "At home I can always smell the least thing burning." She sniffs, as if she can still catch a faint aroma of fuse wire. Nearby, a few other ladies sniff too, and chime loyally: Yes!

"What's with that bigric stuff anyway?" an enormous fellow asks me. A pink blush suffuses his face, as though he were gazing enthusiastically into an Alpine sunset. His "bigric" acid cheers him up as much as popular entertainment might.

A German Nationalist opines that it must have been the work of a Communist. A Communist suspects the German Nationalists. The brimstone smell of a partisan conflict stinks up the air. And all the while, serene and unaware, the Victory Column soars up into the sky, deeply relieved to be barred to visitors.

I am certain that if one could climb the Victory Column now, one would hear God mocking the wickedness and folly of the world, which lives by political partisanship, and dies by picric acid.

—1921

The Prince and the Balalaika

Last Saturday night, the police raided a pub in the west of Berlin and booked eighty Russians and Poles, including four balalaika players. It turned out that a Russian prince and his wife belonged to the barroom quartet. Among the guests were members of the Red Army. The prince told the police that the Bolsheviks had taken away his fortune, leaving him with no option but to try to earn his living by playing the balalaika.

Now, the balalaika is a fine instrument, by no means unworthy of a prince. Not that princes usually went around with their balalaikas in the wine bars of Russia. In Russia, the instrument was generally played by poor singers and traveling musicians, and princes would have to have been in exceptionally good humor to listen to its plinkings with half an ear.

So for the balalaika it is a kind of renaissance to have its strings plucked by princely hands. It corrects an injustice. Then again—

Then again, among the clientele there were members of the Red Army, the power that had expropriated the prince.

In principle, no one can object to members of the Red Army listening to a prince playing music. Only they were sitting in an expensive wine bar, drinking not tea, but wine. And they were not in Russia, but abroad.

From time to time, even a common police report can reveal historical and philosophical connections, show chasms and disclose problems—as is borne out by the raid: Members of the old aristocracy and the new regime sitting in one and the same bar, while the former gagged on the fruits of the Russian Revolution, so refreshing to the latter.

The fruits of revolution are hypertrophic. No historical or psychological analysis of the march of events in Russia will be complete without a chapter on Berlin nightlife, because it is in such bars that the final social conversion of Russian man is enacted. There is no possibility of this happening in Russia—they don't have the bars.

It takes a wine bar to apply the final touch to the listener, the one that allows him to listen to a prince playing music. It takes a wine bar at night to strip the prince of the trappings of class and outfit him with a balalaika.

It is in the wine bars of Berlin, with their rounds of champagne and their clinking glasses, that the will of the Russian people finds its apotheosis. Here, not in Moscow or Petersburg. It is as though the utensils of world history were wine bars. . . .

—1922

The Music Box

There is a beggar who sits in Potsdamer Platz. He has a tiny music box on his knees, a so-called aristonette. When he turns the handle, a metal disk, as full of holes as an Edam cheese, starts to move around and around on top of the box, very slowly. I presume that it makes music. Sometimes, when I'm asleep at home, I can hear a soft and tremulous keening. It's like the sound made by a long single hair when you slide your fingers down it slowly. That's how ghostly these notes are. They pad about on soles of velvet. . . .

Only in my sleep. Potsdamer Platz is very loud. Fiendishly loud. On Potsdamer Platz itself, I hear nothing. I can only see the metal disk rotating. Such a curious and logic-defying phenomenon. An asthmatic music box in—of all places—Potsdamer Platz. It plays doggedly on and won't be quieted. It whimpers and moans, like the other voice of Berlin, the one that goes unheard, unapprehended, all but obliterated by the din of Potsdamer Platz.
—1921

Translated from the German by Michael Hofmann

2

LOTTE JACOBI

MAX BECKMANN

OTTO DIX

GEORGE GROSZ

JOHN HEARTFIELD

JEANNE MAMMEN

CHRISTIAN SCHAD

RAOUL HAUSMANN

FELIX NUSSBAUM

MARSDEN HARTLEY

KARL BLOSSFELDT

LEFT:

Lotte Jacobi, *Erika and Klaus Mann, Berlin,*
1930. Lotte Jacobi Archives, University
of New Hampshire.

RIGHT:

Max Beckmann, *Selbst im Hotel (Self-Portrait
in the Hotel)*, from the series *Voyage to
Berlin*, 1922. Sprengel Museum, Hannover.

Otto Dix, *Grosstadt (Metropolis)*, 1927/28. Galerie der Stadt, Stuttgart.

LEFT:

George Grosz, *Strasse des Vergnügens (Pleasure Street), from Kleine Grosz-Mappe (Small Grosz Portfolio)*, 1917. Berlinische Galerie, Berlin.

RIGHT:

John Heartfield, *S.M. Adolf. Ich führe Euch herrlichen Pleiten entgegen! (His Majesty Adolf. I lead you on to glorious bankruptcy!)*, 1932. Akron Art Museum, Ohio.

S.M. ADOLF

Fotomontage: John Heartfield

Ich
führe Euch herrlichen Pleiten entgegen!

ABOVE:

Raoul Hausmann, *Elasticum*, 1920. Galerie Berinson, Berlin.

RIGHT:

Felix Nussbaum, *Organ Grinder*, 1943. Felix-Nussbaum-Haus,
Kulturgeschichtliches Museum, Osnabrück.

LEFT:

Marsden Hartley, *Portrait*, c. 1914–1915.
Frederick R. Weisman Art Museum, Minneapolis.

ABOVE:

Karl Blossfeldt, *Physostegia virginiana (Virginian False Dragon-head)*,
circa 1900–1920. Friedrich Petzel, New York.

LIBERATING CHAOS:
A CONVERSATION WITH
PETER ZADEK

Peter Zadek's career is, in some ways, a triumph of accident over history— which is to say that the man known in Europe as the "greatest living German director" is a Berlin Jew who left for England in 1933, at the age of seven, studied at Oxford, practiced his craft at the Old Vic School, and returned to Germany only in the late 1950s. Zadek claims to dislike English theater, but his debt to it is enormous. What's "English" about a Zadek play? His evident passion for the actor's art, for performance. What's German? His passion for the director's art, for a transforming vision and the discipline of that vision. What's "Jewish"? Perhaps simply the fact that as an exile, an outsider, he became his own creative country. The signature Zadek is his Merchant of Venice. His Shylock is every Nazi's Aryan fantasy—the blond good looks, the presence, the entitlement. His merchants are every Nazi's stereotype of the stooped and grasping Jew. It's hard to think of another German director who would have had the confidence or distance or even the audacity to imagine a reading of Shakespeare as radical, vivid, and profound as Zadek's.   **Jane Kramer**

The following interview was conducted on April 28, 1999, at Peter Zadek's home in Lucca, Italy.

★ ★ ★

Olivier Ortolani: What is most important to you about directing in the theater today?

Peter Zadek: The most essential aspect of my work has always been the same: the relationship with the actors. Everything else—from the set design to costumes, lights, and music—is secondary. This year I am directing a traveling production of Hamlet, and in my head now the play consists simply of fifteen actors and actresses. My ideal has always been to have a group of traveling players, a troupe of vagabond actors. Until this production, however, I was never successful in making that happen, largely because the best actors today are too bourgeois to just pick up and go. But I would love to work like this all the time.

Olivier Ortolani: When you work with actors, you are known to encourage them to let their imagination go, to take risks and not be afraid of the unknown. What qualities are most important to you in actors and actresses?

Peter Zadek: When I see actors in an audition or on stage and they stir my imagination somehow, then they are interesting to me. If the best actor in the world fails to do this, he doesn't engage me in the least. It usually happens within a few minutes, and it has absolutely nothing to do with the quality of the actor's ability. It sounds completely egocentric on my part, but that's simply the way it is.

As far as I'm concerned, the most important qualities for actors are courage and a certain inner flexibility. Actors must be willing to take everything they find in themselves, and use it as material with no inhibitions. This presumes, of course, a certain level of exhibitionism, but acting is an exhibitionistic profession.

Aside from this, I think that actors must possess an enormous imagination, one that enables them to identify with people and events that exist only in their mind. For example, an actor should be able to imagine flying to the moon while having the most complicated thoughts about Proust. In working with me, it's important that the actor be willing to let me stir and discover his imagination, which is the most difficult aspect. I think many directors are afraid of actors who have this expansive imagination, in part because it is often greater than the director's. One other essential quality is that the actor be able to develop ideas without simplifying them. I need actors who can take what is most

useful from my thoughts, discard the rest, and clarify what is useful until it becomes effective. Theater is not theory, after all, but something that actually happens.

Olivier Ortolani: Having seen some of your productions of Shakespeare and Chekhov, I have the impression that in your eyes the art of acting is at its height when the actors abandon their virtuousity and find their way back to a pure state of curiosity and innocence, a state of openness and abandon that one usually finds only in children.

Peter Zadek: I forget who it was, but someone once said that the best productions of Shakespeare are done by amateurs. Seeing Shakespeare performed by dilettantes has always interested me enormously, just as virtuosity has always bored me, and not only with regard to Shakespeare. That's why, to take just one example, I never liked Peter Brook's famous production of *A Midsummer Night's Dream*. The actors in that production were constantly demonstrating their extraordinary virtuosity, but it was certainly not the virtuosity of a group of circus artists, who may have been able to perform the play much better.

All the artists I find interesting have a very pronounced childlike nature. Naturally, this is a most important element in Shakespeare, because the whole relationship between the actors and the audience in Elizabethan theater was so profoundly direct. One simply said what one meant, and it was received in kind. One also said it very quickly, so that there wasn't really any time to reflect. Today we know that *Hamlet*, performed in its entirety, didn't last any longer than three hours, which is

unthinkable today. It would have to be spoken at a rate which would be impossible to deliver, much less understand, today.

Olivier Ortolani: Where does the richness of Shakespeare lie for you as a director?

Peter Zadek: I think the most striking thing is that it is not a problem to reinterpret Shakespeare every year. There is a certain freedom of movement in Shakespeare's plays that is absolutely extraordinary. I have never encountered another author for whom

this is so true. It really is possible to produce *Hamlet* one way today and then entirely differently six months from now. Both are right or wrong, although this is very difficult to control. What you can control—and this is a bit mysterious—is whether it's Shakespeare or not, which has nothing to do with whether the characters are dressed like Wall Street financiers, as in one of my productions of *The Merchant of Venice*, or in Elizabethan costumes. That is entirely unimportant. Rather, it has to do with understanding Shakespeare's extraordinary imagination.

Olivier Ortolani: In which of your productions of Shakespeare did you get closest to what you had in mind?

Peter Zadek: It is very difficult for me to say, because the answer has to do with where I was during different stages in my development. *The Merchant of Venice* is certainly the one I have produced most often. The play interests me profoundly because I am a Jew, and this is a permanent problem. In what is probably the most famous of these productions, I became fascinated with the artificiality produced by taking Gert Voss, a German actor who is as German as one could possibly imagine—he could easily play an SS officer or Siegfried—and having him play Shylock. I was trying to find a way to make the text seem fresh and original, to get people interested in it again. I thought having someone like Voss play Shylock would wake up the audience, because every line he spoke would sound new, since the expected context for the character would be gone.

Clearly though, one of my best experiences with Shakespeare was the production of *As You Like It* that

I directed in the late seventies. We only played it a few times, and on very small stages in tiny provincial theaters, before an audience of two or three hundred people. These performances had an enormous amount of poetry, intensity, and humor. The audiences were completely under our spell, and the whole thing was pure and wonderful. The actors had no fear, and didn't have to exaggerate their gestures or scream out their lines.

In my opinion the most exciting theater is produced when you have to adapt to a situation, but still manage to transmit the essence of what you're trying to do. That is exactly what happened in those provincial theaters. The various difficulties presented by the different places only made the actors better, whereas the luxury of the richest theaters just made them worse.

Olivier Ortolani: You have often been reproached for exploiting your actors' quirks and whims, and displaying them in an almost voyeuristic way. It seems to me, though, that you explore their eccentricities and mannerisms not to get cheap laughs at their expense, but rather to get at their idiosyncratic, most individual core.

Peter Zadek: You are absolutely right. In the sixties I may very well have exploited my actors a bit, but that was due more to my own ineptness than to my intentions. This was even more true in the seventies, when I put together an ensemble of loonies in Bochum. The most outrageous people in the world were all in Bochum, it seemed. Every day someone with green hair and a nose ring stopped by and said, I belong here, I have to work here. Such a situation has many disadvantages, of course, because after a while you can't do anything conventional anymore. It is also dangerous when the world is no longer recognizable to a conventional audience, and the audience slowly begins to resemble the people on stage. But I have always preferred eccentrics and outsiders. I detest conventional, narrow-minded people, just as I hate petit bourgeois theater. Unfortunately, there are many such theaters in Germany today, and I would count some of the most famous ones among them. Their main problem is that they always aim to be understood by the whole audience, no matter how middlebrow it may be. People must be able to identify with the characters. But when Chekhov's Vanya starts to resemble a Hamburg bank clerk, I am no longer amused.

Olivier Ortolani: Your rehearsals have been described as very chaotic. Is there any danger that actors who are not yet firmly anchored internally might lose their footing and thus their composure, because they can't handle this chaos?

Peter Zadek: Yes, this often happens. My rehearsals are particularly difficult for very experienced and capable actors, because I demand that they give up much of what they have learned. This is difficult for their egos, and can even place their whole existence in question, for if what I'm doing is right, then what they've been doing until then is wrong.

In general though, I have always found it very important not to make order out of the chaos in the actors—a chaos that is also, of course, in myself—but rather to liberate it. I have been working with this tension between chaos and form my entire life. To put it a bit simplistically, I would say that form is what I have found in Germany, and chaos is what I brought with me from England.

Olivier Ortolani: You have said that the Berliner Ensemble's performances in London in the fifties were extraordinarily important to you. How is this true?

Peter Zadek: Above all, what I learned from Brecht was that theater can be intelligent. For all of us in London the Berliner Ensemble's performances were a revelation. We hadn't believed that such a thing was possible. You can't imagine how bleak English theater was during the forties and fifties. Aside from a few extraordinary productions, it was a desert of superficiality. And suddenly we saw these wonderful actors performing with a precision, lucidity, and clarity that we had never experienced before. It was sensational. Because my German wasn't very good at the time, I could only partially understand the plays, and therefore the images and actors have the most prominent place in my memory. Later I read Brecht over and over, trying to find him interesting, but the plays never appealed to me much.

The first Brecht play I directed was *The One Who Says Yes and the One Who Says No* in 1993 at the Berliner Ensemble. This play has always fascinated me because it is the shortest play about revolution. Essentially it suggests that the way to stage a revolution is to say no. I staged only the play then, but I would like to stage the opera as well. Later, when I was offered *Mahagonny*, I became deeply fascinated with Brecht's rather incisive picture of a capitalist world—a world I find unbearable and amoral.

Olivier Ortolani: Your theater has always been one that breaks taboos and unsettles people, but do you find that it gets more and more difficult to provoke shock, outrage, and protest in an audience drawn from our permissive society?

Peter Zadek: Naturally, you can no longer provoke an audience by violating visible and obvious taboos like, to take just one example, sexual taboos. But I

73

find the word "unsettle" too negative. I would prefer to describe what happens as an opening. The point is to bring the audience to an open condition, so that they can move beyond their customary clichés; to do this either consciously or unconsciously, so that they suddenly are somewhere else, and have accepted a reality that they never would have accepted in real life.

Most directors explain too much, and are always looking for answers. I, on the other hand, am always looking for questions. I don't see myself as a philosopher or a professor. The theater is a place where you can ask very pointed questions, where you can present situations that remind the spectators of things they wouldn't have thought about otherwise. As a spectator I want to be asked for my opinion, but I certainly don't want to have someone lecturing me.

Olivier Ortolani: Many of your productions have been rather controversial, but what do you think it is that causes the most offense?

Peter Zadek: I think it's the way I see and present the world as a place of constant flux, motion, and anarchy.

Olivier Ortolani: What do you think contemporary theater suffers from most?

Peter Zadek: Certainly not from too little money or from the fact, as many people in the theater believe, that no one wants to go to the theater any more. In Germany the most interesting theaters have always originated in situations where there was no money at all. I think that the theater—definitely in Germany, but really all over Europe—is out of step with contemporary developments in art as well as life. At the moment we are in a sort of intermediate phase, a difficult period in which theater is trying to reorient itself. But we forge ahead with our work. I'm always searching.

Translated from the German by Ilka Saal

PAGES 66 AND 69:
Angela Winkler in a rehearsal of Peter Zadek's production of *Hamlet*, Strasbourg, May 1999.

PAGES 70 AND 72:
Rehearsal of Peter Zadek's *The Merchant of Venice*, Vienna, June 1989.

PAGE 71:
Eva Mattes, Gert Voss and Peter Zadek in a rehearsal of *The Merchant of Venice*, Vienna, June 1989.

THE
LEFT SHOE

FELICITAS HOPPE

EVERYBODY SAYS POTSDAMER PLATZ, Potsdamer Platz, everybody talks about it endlessly, but I for one have never seen it. I've lived in this city for years, I've crossed it many nights while drunk, or just having been drunk, from north to south, from east to west, but not once have I seen Potsdamer Platz. Everybody says look for the angel, the golden angel on the Victory Column, and then walk straight ahead, but I always go in circles until the angel, exhausted from being looked at all the time, finally saves itself and drops its wreath onto the next available head—my sister's. We've often played this game when it was late at night and we couldn't think of anything else to do. My sister would grab some object off the shelf—a book, a vase containing flowers, a camera without film—you're the angel, she'd cry, here's your wreath, and I'd hold it up in the air, standing on my tiptoes, while my sister sleepily counted the seconds. My arm leaden, I never held out for more than three minutes, and my sister would laugh because she could do it longer.

But she hates this city. She comes here only once every two years, and then it's because of me. She puts her suitcase by the door, says the city is imaginary, and won't leave her spot on the sofa until her departure. From there she watches me restlessly roaming the city day and night—during, after and before bouts of drunkenness—and sometimes, out of despair, joining groups of visitors as they wander the streets, led by knowledgeable guides. These guides are always holding something in the air—a tattered city map, pennants, banners, or an umbrella destroyed by the local rainstorms, with a dirty handkerchief attached to its tip. I can recognize the guides from far off, but I can't understand what they're saying because their voices are thin and worn. All the same, when there's a burst of laughter I laugh, like the visitors, although they don't know why they're laughing either, because the men are busy poking the girls hurrying past in the ribs, and the women are opening purses and holding pocket mirrors up to their faces. I know just how the fleeing girls' ribs crack and what's in the women's pockets, and still I've never seen Potsdamer Platz.

But I haven't given up. I keep looking for cranes and pennants, for the group that will one day take me to Potsdamer Platz before I end up losing them again. I always lose them, because I don't look like a tourist. My step is all too decisive, as if I know where I'm going, so that people like to take my arm gently and ask in a whisper whether there was once a wall here too. And though I can't remember, no matter how hard I try, I get a piece of chalk out of my pocket at once and decisively draw a line between my feet one more time, between left foot and right foot, from south to north or from east to west, wherever you like—right on the pavement, right where you're standing. And although it's a fraud, as even my sister could tell from the sofa, the visitors give me money, so I know that they love it.

Later I took a taxi to Potsdamer Platz with that money. I thought I could see it from far away. I called and waved, but the driver didn't turn. He kept driving in a circle and was quiet as a fish. I gave him the fare and got out. A woman was sitting on the curb, crying. She wasn't very pretty, and had lost her group and the heel on her left shoe, which she held up in the air reproachfully, and her left foot was hovering just off the ground, because it's very dirty here and it often rains, which results, my sister says, from the fact that people always wear the wrong shoes here. She doesn't wear heels herself, nor does she know pity.

But I got some chalk out of my pocket, and a bottle, which I held up to the woman's lips. She drank promptly, then she was still. Then she was happy, and I drank too and was also happy. We drew lines, streets, and squares, until right before our eyes the city dissolved on the pavement, because it was wet and dark. The woman's left foot was still hovering in the darkness above the street. In one hand she was holding the shoe, in the other the bottle, holding herself upright, and I sleepily counted the seconds until the bottle was finally empty and her arm sank slowly down. And although this story is made up, as my sister knows right away, I have to tell it to her again and again, for it's very

late, and we are much too tired to grab objects off the shelf, or call a taxi and
drive around in circles for so long that the angel is finally moved, and throws
her wreath onto the head of the woman, who gets up, teeters, steps into the
brightly lit square, and holds a shoe up in the air. We know this well, we've
played it often, just like this: If it's the right shoe, my sister loses, takes her
suitcase, and leaves. If it's the left shoe, she wins twice, for I have to leave
with her, and I still haven't seen Potsdamer Platz.

Translated from the German by Andrew Shields

3

ARWED MESSMER

HEIDI SPECKER

DOUG HALL

JOHN MILLER

ARWED MESSMER: CITY IN PASSAGE

For many years Arwed Messmer has photographed Berlin, focusing on the cracks in the architectural fabric: the city's construction sites and empty lots. Berlin celebrates its construction sites as *Schaustellen*, "observation sites." They are publicly accessible and even have their own museum: the Infobox at Potsdamer Platz. Every architectural competition is presented in an exhibition, and a large scale model of "Berlin 2000" is an integral part of every tourist tour. In Messmer's photographs, these views become scenes and the people actors, as if staged to locate the image in the present moment.

The workers in Messmer's photograph of Freidrichstrasse's Quartier 206 define the image's foreground and orient it. Visitors attending a ground-breaking ceremony at Potsdamer Platz structure the scene and turn it into a society portrait that shows the reconstruction of Berlin not as a spectacle, but as a matter of public interest.

Messmer's view is neither a glorification of the old nor a celebration of the new. His photographs are tableaux of a society, revealing the brief moments that occur between the historic city and the reinvented city, foreboding panoramas that counteract the strategic tendency to let massive changes in the urban fabric appear harmless. His works necessitate a critical participation, and they share with nineteenth-century Parisian "paintings of modern life" the conception of a public sphere that is based on compassion.

Christian Rattemeyer

Arwed Messmer, *City #06*, 1994.

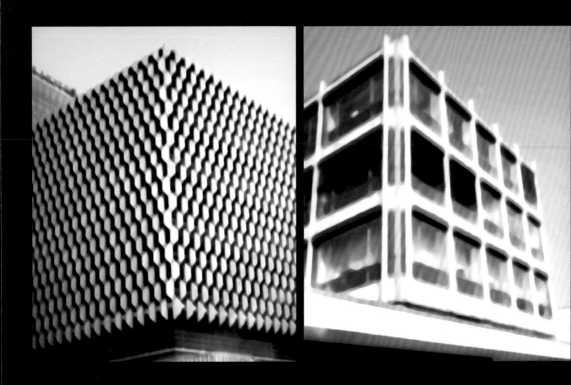

Heidi Specker. (left) *Alexanderplatz,* **(right)** *Philips.* From the series *Speckergruppen Bildings,* 1995.

Doug Hall, *Congress Hall of the Volkskammer Palast der Republik, Berlin,* from the series *The GDR Project,* 1992.

John Miller, *Untitled (8.26.95)*, 1995.

TRANSIT BERLIN

DURS GRÜNBEIN

for Sergei K., the first hostage in orbit

What a nightmare—someone's orbiting around up there in the universe, alone in his capsule crammed full of electronics, a Russian cosmonaut, a hermit in orbit, shot by other members of his species into space, where no one can hear him scream. Time passes differently up there than down on the earth, and after a hundred or more days, when he comes back, everything has changed, as if overnight. The world he finds is different than the world before the launch. Several small revolutions and great putsches have come to pass. The superpower, the seventy-year-old construct that was his nation, has fallen apart, as has the whole hierarchy of the state apparatus; the government and the political system have disintegrated. His previous patrons have vanished from the control centers. The army to which service regulations say he belongs is under new command. Nothing is familiar to him anymore, even the national currency is new, and portraits of leaders and monuments to heroes have been swept away throughout the country with a frenzy that has already blown over. Einstein's relativity, the duality or infinite multiplicity of times unwinding alongside each other—all at once it's a trivial experience he can hold in his hands.

Nietzsche's vision, the revaluation of all values, forgetting as the irruption of the vegetative into historical time, suddenly confronts him at the end of a long journey into the galactic night. From the moment he sets foot on native soil again, everything is different. Weren't static worldly relationships, the permafrost of the real, long the basis for the success of so many exorbitant projects, just as the immovable launching pad guaranteed the acceleration of the rocket? What an equation of times, inner and outer, eastern and western, worldly and interplanetary—a whole world collapses when this temporal structure loosens or shifts by just a matter of seconds, or seconds of arc. But isn't this exactly what happened with the fall of the Soviet empire? Didn't a supernova just appear in the skies of history? An earthquake of 10.0 on the Richter scale has occurred in Europe, and suddenly entire populations feel just like that solitary man returning from space. The ground has grown shaky underfoot. As if from distant sanctuaries, a new architecture has long been rising—accelerating more rapidly with every postwar decade—toward the dazed observer, along with a development plan and a semiotics. The static topography of Eastern Europe, deeply engraved in the senses and memories of its inhabitants, is giving way to the dynamic, cyclical world of the West, with all its centrifugal forces—economic, political, and moral. Like an old picture tube, space implodes behind the time-lapsed breakup of the closed horizon, the typical Campanella infrastructure, its surface grid formed by walls, borders, huts, suburban developments, and barracks. The emigration of icons and unrealizable visions is followed by the importation of goods and values. And the East, too, finally sees the dawn of the polytheistic age with its new people, who, as Paul Valéry had already foreseen in 1940, "will leap through religions as if they were paper tires."

What was different, one wonders today, about those people on the other side of the magic line; how different were their everyday lives, their thinking, and their culture? Did they sleep through time in monotonous cycles and paranoid isolation? Are their biographies only now, with the breaking of the time barrier and the dissolution of the status quo, flowing back into the great general stream of history? And what does artistic work mean twenty thousand leagues under the sea, down on the deep-sea bottom, or up in some orbit in eschatological time? Were any of the survivors of Orwellian states able to maintain their single-mindedness, amid megalomania, cynicism, self-surrender, and banal ideals, amid sunken social strata and against all collective tectonics? Of course some were, but what influence can their strength have in a phase when necrophilic recollection has long been wrestling with animalistic forgetting?

If it is true that the large-scale social experiment in the East has produced a different anthropological type, then Berlin more than any other place in Europe is predestined to confirm it. For here lies the key to the absurd juxtaposition of two times, two models, two ways of being as different from each other as those of natives and missionaries in the age of the voyages of discovery.

It was here, after all, that new types stepped out on the catwalks of the cabaret in the twenties. It was one of the most spectacular urban shows of its time, with the radar human, the engineer of souls, the androgynous stage star, the nerve clown, the urban philosopher—figments of a newly objective imagination, between the ages of silent and sound films. They all disappeared, like vampires in a shower of holy water, on the Nazi Ash Wednesday, at a single word from the Führer, and have never been seen since. Even today, there are some who mourn this past's great phantoms, which no economic miracle, no postwar blessing, and certainly no collective camp life could ever revive. Neither under the Allied protectorate in the western part of the city nor under the strict supervisory eye of Stalin's Communist bishops in the eastern part was an aesthetic renaissance on such a scale possible.

Berlin—all terror came from here. This was the eye of the cyclone, where an evil windless calm long ruled, until this place, too, a breeding ground for the spirits of destruction, was laid waste and subdued by bomber formations from the West and tanks from the East, and then contractually divided up among enemies and placed under guardianship. After that, hysteria ruled the city, the competition of market and Marx. More than once it seemed as if the Third World War would be sparked off here, at the system gates between East and West. The weary dualism, the madness of good and evil, could be felt in each body, each brain, becoming with the years a geographical-political-anatomical rift that no biography, no worldview, and no aesthetic project could escape. But who was a piece in the game, and who was a witness? Who had the comfort of inner distance, of the guiding ideological concepts of Left or Right, and who was a hostage in the scenario of the powers? Was the West's sensitivity the slow East? Was the East's futility the dynamic West? And did anything flourish outside the division of the world, in philosophical-historical terms, into will (West) and representation (East)?

It's time to talk about the situation of the artist today, after reunification. Of course, only anecdotes —for the most part unbelievable stories—can reproduce what happened here during the years of real division. Nothing will explain why the city's art had to be declared missing. No series of documentaries on the Wall being built, or on blockades, smear campaigns, worker uprisings, student demonstrations, and spy exchanges—not a single motif from this Cold War panorama can say anything about the modes of its disappearance. And only the old can say what is really missing, if only to have to hear the young tell them what has, thank God, been sold off cheaply, and what has landed in the garbage. For in the nakedness, in the barren symmetry of East and West, in all the coldness of a frontline city, the twisted gap between the generations still persists. Against the nostalgic monologues rustling like wastepaper across empty squares, against the phantom pain left behind by streets erased, by life-worlds flattened, by cemeteries covered with rubble—against all this and more, young people offer their OK, their appetite for fashions, technologies, and concepts— and there it is, almost cynical. Are they really the first to have recognized that identity is a picture puzzle, the sum of individual illusions, together amounting to nothing but a popular phantasm? The no-man's-lands, the intermediate zones, the still unmarked areas—these, it seems, are now their hunting grounds. Here, clowns of the virtual, they cultivate the existence of someone living in a space

of transit. Their secret credo is openness in all directions, a compulsive vigilance in the middle of a physical world where the self is dismantled and dissolved into a million pieces by a multiplicity of stimuli. The new artist no longer has a program, just nerves and a fine nose for coordinates. Tropisms at the edges of old forms, indifferent steps, and leaps into the immaterial are the favorite moves in this game, which is perpetually abandoning rules and making new ones. Style is no more than ironically playful disguise or mimicry, a series of insectlike movements in the twilight of greenhouse afternoons. This artist's path is a zigzag through the urban danger zones, no different than that followed by bands of kids passing their time with car chases, subway surfing, or department store piracy. Flight, breakdown, stuttering, little aesthetic aphasias—it's always the defect, the disturbance in the social process, the laughable, intelligible adventure that stimulates him. In the eyes of these drifters, whatever once guaranteed exclusivity—style, theme, grand gestures, expression—is taboo, a necrophilic, passé pleasure. Can it be merely a coincidence that they all travel so often? They're a generation of jet-setters, perpetually on the move, busy comparing clocks and translating from one sphere to the next, nowhere at home and never arriving. Berlin is the best location for their film, with its infinite layers of images; it's a kind of reality studio hastily furnished by two superpowers, a Hollywood made of replacement parts from the hot spots of European history, a Prussian–Protestant–Socialist *Cinecittà* of boulevards, courtyards, central offices, villas, museums, and railroad networks. Berlin is absurdly peppered with tiny traps in even its smallest niches or, in many places, where the Brandenburg sand is exposed, simply swept superficially clean, the ideal place for backdrops. At this turning point between Eastern and Western Europe, they wake up, the first to have the new vertigo characteristic of the transit artist, elsewhere long since the standard type. In our latitudes, they are the first to return from that long nightmare called history.

Transitio—it always meant three things in Latin, and the fine distinctions deposited in and alternately emerging from this single word might shed some light on its contemporary variations. First, it meant going over to the enemy, a genuine Roman trauma. In the class theory still valid just moments ago, this part of the Eastern artist's task has been fulfilled, whether of necessity or of his own initiative. He has now arrived right where a regime pedagogically intent on isolation could only have considered him lost. Moving from the political to the pathological, the second meaning is infection with an illness. If dynamism, efficiency, libidinous idiocy, and technology are seen as specifically Western forms of disease, this requirement will soon be fulfilled, too, even if there are a few who still stay on their diet and long to go back to some village out of the last century. The most omnipresent meaning, however, so physically basic that it concerns each individual body, defines transitio as passage through a place. In an age of absolute acceleration and medialization, this is presumably the true movement. Early familiarity with the media (themselves transitory, or non-places), the transience of all efforts, the eye-catching gatherings, especially those at transitional points and interfaces—all this behavior, which can only be understood zoologically, along a straight line from point A (birth) to point B (death), presages the breakneck speed at which the change will be completed. Today, as paradoxical as it may sound, the artist is only comprehensible at certain

points; the larger part of the artist's work, whether it is immaterial or strategically scattered around the globe, either remains on the run or has long since made its way into the physical, everyday world. Nothing would be more ridiculous than to keep talking about an oeuvre, what with all the temporary installations, invisible field studies, and the found objects briefly exhibited before being immediately put back into circulation. No matter how well-founded, reprocessed, and humorously or pompously presented in museums it may seem, all this is at best a selection, a stopgap, a brief pause in the barrage of reproduction, or a fleeting piece of evidence, cunningly lifted from an anonymous semantics. Linguistically it has lost all coherence, precisely because of its polyvalence. As fragment, event, arbitrary act, or statement by a solitary voice in the babble, however, it lays claim to being a *moment juste.* "Prick up your ears and go on" could be the slogan of all the friendly participants. For in the transitory, no discourse survives beyond the next name change, the next collapse of hierarchy. Have we now finally arrived at a place where, one hundred years ago, Nietzsche saw intellect and art stirring, in an empire of signs and illusion, where the "free lie" plays with the elements of a world increasingly dissolving into its changing appearances?

Translated from the German by Andrew Shields

SARAH KIRSCH

Raw Medley

But what's nicest of all: with you
Or without you
Roaming the boulevards nothing in my bag
But raisin bread, wine, and tobacco
Keeping the people from distant countries
In view and later
Discussing them, describing the sky the snow
You come with the west wind and I
From the north, we collect
All that, the tiny horses
The vertical palm trees, the stars, coffeemakers
In the afternoons half past four, when the bell
Swings and screams in the cage

Translated from the German by Peter Constantine

INGE MÜLLER   **The Way Home 45**

Left over accidentally
I walk the familiar way
From one end of the city to the other end
Free of the hated uniform
Hiding in stolen clothes
Upright, if the fear is too much
Crawling across the dead with no face
The fallen city watches me
I look away. Beside me five children argue
Over a bag of bank notes:
At the corner the bank is being looted
Those who never could save occupy the savings and loan
Stuffing their hollow clothes with crumpled paper
Against the cold.
The dream of bread circulates, emboldening those frozen by fear
Propelling the slow onward
Not letting the victors rest on the victory
And the vanquished open wide their hands:
Who is the price, who will set the price
We?
Left over accidentally
I walk the way home from one end of the city
To the other end.

Translated from the German by Matthew Griffin

BERLIN'S SKELETON IN UTAH'S CLOSET

MIKE DAVIS

BERLIN'S MOST FAR-FLUNG, secret and orphan suburb sits in the saltbush desert about ninety miles southwest of Salt Lake City. "German Village," as it is officially labeled on declassified maps of the U.S. Army's Dugway Proving Ground, is the remnant of a much larger, German-Japanese composite "doom town" constructed by Standard Oil in 1943. Dugway played a crucial role in the New Deal's last great public works project: the incineration of cities in eastern Germany and Japan.

Two years ago, the Army allowed me to tour German Village briefly with a dozen of my students from the Southern California Institute of Architecture. Dugway is slightly bigger than Rhode Island and more toxically contaminated than the Nuclear Test Site in nearby Nevada. As the devil's own laboratory for three generations of U.S. chemical, incendiary, and biological weapons, it has always been shrouded in official secrecy and Cold War myth. A recent threat of base restructuring, however, has prompted the Army to mount a small public relations campaign on Dugway's behalf. Since napalm, botulism and binary nerve gas are not conventional tourist attractions, the Proving Ground instead advertises its preservation of an original section of the Lincoln Highway. Most visitors are pioneering motorists who come to admire the decrepit, one-lane bridge that crosses a swampy patch in Baker Area, not far from the controversial bio-warfare lab where the Army tinkers with andromeda strains, guarded by a double perimeter of razor wire. German Village is a dozen or so miles further west, in a sprawling maze of mysterious test sites and target areas that Dugway's commander is reluctant to include on the visitor itinerary. He relented only when we convinced his press office that the Village had an important aesthetic aura that might enhance "base heritage": it was designed by one of Modernism's gods, the German-Jewish architect Eric Mendelsohn.

Burning Berlin's Red Districts

In 1943, the Chemical Warfare Corps secretly recruited Mendelsohn to work with Standard Oil engineers to create a miniature Hohenzollern slum in the Utah desert. Nothing in the appearance of the surviving structure—a double tenement block known as Building 8100—identifies it as the product of the same hand that designed such landmarks of Weimar Berlin as the offices of the *Berliner Tageblatt*, the Columbushaus, the Sternefeld villa in Charlottenburg, or the Woga Complex on the Kurfürstendamm. Absolute "typicality" in all aspects of layout and construction was what the Chemical Warfare Corps wanted. They were in a hurry. Despite the horrifying success of their thousand-bomber fire raids against Cologne and Hamburg in mid-1943, the Allies were increasingly frustrated by their inability to ignite a firestorm in the Reich capital. Their top science advisers urged a crash program of incendiary experimentation on exact replicas of working-class housing. (The design and construction processes were planned to dovetail with secret research on the flammability of Japanese homes.) Only the United States—or, rather, the combined forces of Hollywood and the oil industry—had the resources to complete the assignment in a few months.

Mendelsohn's achievement was the anonymity of his result: six iterations of the steeply gabled brick tenements—*Mietskasernen*, or rent barracks—that made the Red districts of Berlin the densest slums in Europe. Three of the apartment blocks had tile on batten roofs, characteristics of Berlin construction, while the other three had slate over sheathing roofs, more commonly found in the factory cities of the Ruhr. Although not as tall as their seven-story counterparts in Wedding or Kreuzberg, the test structures were otherwise astonishingly precise simulacra.

Before drawing any blueprints, Mendelsohn exhaustively researched the roof area—a critical incendiary parameter—of target neighborhoods in Berlin and other industrial cities. His data was "extended and confirmed," reported the Standard Oil Development Company, "by a member of the Harvard Architecture School, an expert on German wooden frame building construction." (Could it have been Walter Gropius?) The builders, working with fire protection engineers, gave extraordinary attention to ensuring that the frames (made with authentic woods, imported from as far away as Murmansk) duplicated the aging and specific density of older German construction. When the fire experts objected that Dugway's climate was too arid, their Standard Oil counterparts contrived to keep the level of wood moisture accurate by having GIs regularly "water" the target, to simulate Prussian rain.

The interior furnishing, meanwhile, was subcontracted to RKO Radio Pictures' Authenticity Division, the wizards behind *Citizen Kane*. Using German-trained craftsmen, they duplicated the cheap but heavy furniture that was the dowry of Berlin's proletarian households. German linen was carefully studied to ensure the typicality of bed coverings and drapes. While the authenticators debated details with Mendelsohn and the fire engineers, the construction process was secretly accelerated by the wholesale conscription of inmates from the Utah State Prison. It took them only forty-four days to complete German Village and its Japanese counterpart (twelve double apartments fully furnished with hinoki and tatami). The entire complex was then firebombed and completely reconstructed at least three times between May and September of 1943.

Mendelsohn's secret signature on German Village is rich in irony. Like all of his progressive Weimar contemporaries, he had a deep interest in housing reform and the creation of a *neue Wohnkultur* (new culture of living). Yet, as his biographers have noted, he was never involved in the big social housing competitions organized by the Social Democrats in the late 1920s, which were such crucial showcases for the urbanist ideas of the emergent modern movement. His absence was most dramatic (and mysterious) in the case of the 1927 *Weissenhof Siedlung*—the model housing project coordinated by Mies van der Rohe and sponsored by Stuttgart's left-wing government—which Philip Johnson has called "the most important group of buildings in the history of modern architecture." In Mendelsohn's biography, Bruno Zevi suggests that Mendelsohn was "excluded from the large works of the *Siedlungen*" because of anti-Semitism.

If so, Dugway was his revenge. Here was workers' housing perversely designed to accelerate the campaign "to dehouse the German industrial worker," as the British bluntly put it. The Weissenhof masterpieces of Gropius and the Taut brothers were among the 45 percent of the 1939 German housing stock that Bomber Command and the Eighth Air Force managed to destroy or damage by the spring of 1945. (Indeed, Allied bombers pounded into rubble more 1920s socialist and modernist utopias than they did Nazi villas.)

Did Mendelsohn and the other anti-Nazi refugees who worked on German Village have qualms about incendiary experimentation that involved only plebeian housing? Did they apprehend the terror and agony that the Chemical Warfare Corps was meticulously planning to inflict upon the Berlin proletariat? No memoir or correspondence—Mendelsohn was notoriously tight-lipped—offers any information. Historians of the U.S. Air Force, on the other hand, have excavated a complex, sometimes tortured debate (as never occurred in the racial inferno of the Pacific theater) over the ethics of firebombing Berlin.

The Zoroastrian Society

During the early days of the Second World War, tens of millions of American voters of German and Italian ancestry were reassured that the U.S. Air Force would never deliberately make a target out of "the ordinary man in the street." In every region but the East—where, as Curtis Le May would later tell his Tokyo-bound pilots, "there are no civilians"—Americans (in 1943, as in 1999) were officially committed to the clean, high-tech destruction of strictly military or military-industrial targets. The Eighth Air Force sent its crews in daylight "precision" raids against visually identified targets, in contrast to its Blitz-embittered British allies, who saturation-bombed German cities at night, hoping to terrorize their populations into flight or rebellion. The extraordinary technologies of the B-17 and the Norden bombsight allowed the United States to bomb "with democratic values." (Then as now, "collateral damage" was smugly swept under the national conscience.)

But, as the construction of German Village dramatizes, the story is considerably more sinister. While military doctrine, aircraft technology, and sensitivity to domestic public opinion ensured a huge investment in precision bombing, counter-civilian or "morale" bombing had never been excluded from U.S. war planning against Germany. Indeed, as Ronald Schaffer and other historians have shown, AWPD 1—the secret strategy for an air war against Germany that was adopted months before Pearl Harbor—specifically envisioned that it might be "highly profitable to deliver a large-scale, all-out attack on the civil population of Berlin" after precision bombing had disrupted Ruhr industries.

The British, moreover, fiercely pressured the U.S. Eighth Air Force to join their "area bombing"

95

crusade. Churchill, encouraged by his chief science adviser and Dr. Strangelove, Lord Cherwell, had turned to terror bombing in March of 1942 less out of revenge for the Blitz (although this ensured strong public support) than from the idée fixe that civilian morale was Germany's Achilles heel. Although a case might have been made for singling out the homes of the Nazi political and industrial elites for aerial punishment, this risked retaliation against Burke's Peerage and had thus been excluded by Cherwell from the onset. ("The bombing must be directed essentially against working-class houses. Middle-class houses have too much space around them, and so are bound to waste bombs.") Thus the squalid Mietskasernen were ground zero. And by November 1942, when thousand-bomber night raids had become common over western Germany, Churchill was able to share with his allies the optimistic quotas that the Royal Air Force had pledged to produce: nine hundred thousand civilians dead, one million seriously injured, and twenty-five million homeless.

If some of the U.S. precision bombers, such as General George McDonald, the director of Air Force intelligence, were appalled by this descent to "indiscriminate homicide and destruction," there is evidence that the commander in chief, influenced by his own Strangelovian advisers, had a more open mind about massacring enemy civilians. When the RAF's Operation Gomorrah succeeded in kindling tornadic firestorms in the heart of Hamburg in July and August of 1943 (seven thousand children were among the carbonized victims), Roosevelt was reportedly greatly impressed.

Gomorrah also strengthened the hand of the fire war advocates within the Army Air Force and the National Defense Research Committee. In England,

the RAF had organized an informal discussion group, the so-called Zoroastrian Society, to share expertise on incendiaries with Eighth Air Force planners. It soon became an intellectual home for aggressive young commanders like Curtis Le May, who were infected with the British enthusiasm for incendiary weapons and wanted to see their deployment greatly expanded. (Incendiaries, all sides agreed, were most effective against civilian housing, not industry or infrastructure.)

On the home front, the firebombing of Axis capitals enjoyed powerful support from influential Harvard scientists (led by the "father of napalm," chemist Louis Feiser), the oil companies, and the fire protection industry. The fire insurance experts, one historian points out, "did not simply advise the Army Air Force. They pushed it as hard as they could to make it wage incendiary warfare against factories and homes." They loved to point out to airmen the overlooked fire potentials of structures like churches, which were "quite vulnerable to small incendiaries."

German Village was constructed in May 1943, on the eve of Churchill's burnt offering at Hamburg, to address opportunities and problems that were beyond the moral boundary of precision bombing. It was a trade show for the burgeoning fire war lobby. Those planning the coming air war against Japan were eager to see how new incendiaries, including napalm and an incredible "bat bomb" that released hundreds of live bats booby-trapped with tiny incendiary devices, performed against Dugway's Japanese houses. Meanwhile, the Zoroastrian Society was looking for clues on how to burn up Berlin's massive masonry shell.

Churchill's "Morale Bombing"

In his authoritative report on "The Fire Attacks on German Cities," Horatio Bond, the National Defense Research Committee's chief incendiary expert, underscored the Allies' frustration. "Berlin was harder to burn than most of the other German cities. There was better construction and better 'compartmentation.' In other words, residential buildings did not present themselves as large fire divisions or fire areas. Approximately twice as many incendiaries had to be dropped to assure a fire in each fire division." As the German Village tests clarified, "little [could] be expected in the way of the free spread of fire from building to building." Buildings were lost "because they were hit by bombs rather than because fire spread from other buildings."

Yet until Zhukov was literally spitting in the Spree, the British clung to the belief (or dementia, as many Americans saw it) that Berlin could be bombed out of the war. Although the Mietskasernen were not easily combustible, RAF planners argued that this could be compensated for with more bombers and greater incendiary density. British strategy was built upon the assumption that intolerable civilian suffering would inevitably produce a proletarian revolt in the heart of the Third Reich. (In this sense, Churchill had more faith in Marxist doctrine than Stalin, who alone seemed to understand the enormity of Hitlerism's moral hold on the capital.) When the RAF's costly reverse blitz failed to incite Berliners against the Führer, Churchill cajoled Roosevelt into unleashing an American "super-raid"—a deus ex machina that also failed.

Armageddon was thus produced in two acts: the RAF's Battle of Berlin in November of 1943, and the Eighth Air Force's "Operation Thunderclap" in February of 1945. Promising the British people that "Berlin will be bombed until the heart of Nazi Germany ceases to beat," Sir Arthur "Bomber" Harris unleashed the RAF's heavy bombers on November 18. In a new strategy that the Germans dubbed *Bombenteppich*, or carpet bombing, the Lancasters, flying in dangerously tight formations, concentrated their bomb loads on small, densely populated areas. Incendiary attacks were followed by explosives, dropped with the deliberate aim of killing firefighters and rescue workers. In accordance with the RAF's doctrine of targeting Weimar's red belts to maximize discontent, the famous Communist stronghold of Wedding was thoroughly pulverized and firebombed.

The zoo was also a major target, which inadvertently increased the meat ration of the city's poorer residents. "Berliners discovered to their surprise that some unusual dishes were extremely tasty. Crocodile tail, for instance, cooked slowly in large containers, was not unlike fatty chicken, while bear ham and sausages proved a particular delicacy." Although Harris was unable to fuel a Hamburg-style firestorm in the Tiergarten, the Lancasters did flatten almost a quarter of the metropolitan core. The BBC boasted that as many as one million Berliners had been killed or injured.

Yet as Harris himself had to acknowledge to Churchill, the RAF's all-out effort "did not appear to be an overwhelming success." For one thing, Goebbels, the city's real ruler, mounted a brilliant defense with his flak towers, squadrons of deadly night fighters, and fire brigades conscripted from all over Germany. Five percent of the British aircrews were shot out of the sky every night, an unsustainable sacrifice for Bomber Command. Moreover, despite terrible damage to the slums, the real machinery of power and production in Berlin remained remarkably undamaged. Strategic bombing analysts marveled at the ability of the city's industries "to produce war material in scarcely diminished quantities almost up to the end."

Goebbels cunningly shifted the parameters of the Allies' calculus of German suffering. More than one million nonessential civilians, especially children, were sent into the countryside, while hundreds of thousands of Russian and Polish prisoners of war were moved directly under Allied bombsights. While Hitler was throwing tantrums in his bunker, Goebbels was holding stirring rallies in the ruins, harvesting populist anger produced by the carpet bombing of working-class neighborhoods. At the same time, he massively reinforced his sprawling network of surveillance and terror— ensuring that any seed of discontent would be promptly destroyed before it could germinate into a larger conspiracy. The British, meanwhile, were seemingly oblivious to the possibility that "morale bombing" was actually strengthening the Nazi state.

Indeed, the RAF clung with striking fanaticism to its flawed paradigm. Harris convinced Churchill that "we can [still] wreck Berlin from end to end if the U.S. Air Force will come in on it." In the winter and spring of 1944, as the sensational new long-range fighters began to give American B-17s unprecedented protection over eastern Germany, the Eighth Air Force, while still theoretically selecting only precision targets, joined British area bombers in a series of thousand-plane raids on Berlin, predictably culminating with a second carpet bombing of Wedding and its red sister, Pankow. One and a half million Berliners were made homeless, but industrial output, again, quickly rebounded.

Operation Thunderclap

Roosevelt had thus far in the war reconciled the divergent philosophies of strategic bombing by accepting, at the 1943 Casablanca Conference, the British concept of a Combined Bomber Offensive "to undermine the morale of the German people," while at the same time preserving the Army Air Force's tactical option for daylight, precision targets. After Hitler retaliated for D-Day with his V-1 and then V-2 attacks on London, this compromise became untenable. Indeed, Churchill's initial reaction to Germany's secret weapons was to demand poison gas attacks or worse on Berlin: "It is absurd to consider morality on this topic," he hectored RAF planners in early July. "I want the matter studied in cold blood by sensible people, and not by psalm-singing, uniformed defeatists."

As Barton Bernstein has shown, Churchill asked Roosevelt to speed up the delivery of five hundred thousand top-secret "N-bombs" containing deadly anthrax, which had been developed at Dugway's Granite Peak complex. The RAF, writes Bernstein, "was putting together a plan for the use of anthrax against six German cities: Berlin, Hamburg, Stuttgart, Frankfurt, Aachen, and Wilhelmshafen. The expectation was that forty thousand of the 500-pound projectiles, containing about 4.25 million four-pound bombs, would kill at least half the population by inhalation, and many more would die later through skin absorption.

Poison gas and anthrax were too much for the White House, but Roosevelt passionately wanted to offer something to the British. In August 1944, he complained angrily to his Secretary of Treasury, Henry Morgenthau, Jr.: "We have got to be tough with Germany, and I mean the German people, not just the Nazis. We either have to castrate the German people or treat them in such a manner that they can't just go on reproducing people who want to continue the way they have in the past." The same month, Churchill offered Roosevelt an RAF plan, Operation Thunderclap, that would guarantee to "castrate" 275,000 Berliners (dead and injured) with a single two thousand-bomber super-raid against the city center. Roosevelt, following Chief of Staff George Marshall's advice, accepted the plan in principle.

Some key Air Force leaders were disturbed by the unsavory implications of Thunderclap. Major General Laurence Kuter protested to colleagues that "it is contrary to our national ideals to wage war against civilians." Lieutenant General Carl Spaatz, the commander of the U.S. bombers in Europe, had "no doubt . . . that the RAF wants very much to have the U.S. Air Forces tarred with the morale bombing aftermath, which we feel will be terrific." War hero Jimmy Doolittle, the Eighth Air Force commander, also remonstrated bitterly after being ordered by Eisenhower, in September of 1944, to be ready to drop bombs "indiscriminately" on Berlin.

Nor did Air Force commanders in Europe necessarily buy the argument of Washington planners, who thought Stalin had grown too omnipotent on the battlefield and needed a compelling demonstration of the destructive power of Allied bombers. The RAF Air Staff had added this frosting to Thunderclap's cake in an August 1944 briefing: "A spectacular and final object lesson to the German people on the consequences of

universal aggression would be of continuing value in the postwar period. Again, the total devastation of the center of a vast city such as Berlin would offer incontrovertible proof to all peoples of the power of a modern air force. . . . It would convince our Russian allies and the Neutrals of the effectiveness of Anglo-American air power."

In the end, Thunderclap (which now included Dresden and Leipzig on its agenda) was unleashed for competing and contradictory reasons, having as much to do with starting the Cold War as with ending the Second World War. Meanwhile, the potential of what American planners called "promiscuous bombardment" had been dramatically increased by the influx of hundreds of thousands of panicked refugees fleeing the advancing Red Army in early 1945. When the leaden winter skies finally cleared over Berlin on February 3, Doolittle stubbornly withheld his more vulnerable B-24s, but sent in nine hundred B-17s and hundreds of fighter escorts. It was not the knockout blow that the British had envisioned, but twenty-five thousand Berliners nonetheless perished, while deep under the burning Reich Chancellery, Hitler listened to Wagner.

Dresden, a month later, was closer to the original, apocalyptic conception of Thunderclap. Crowded with refugees, slave laborers and Allied prisoners, the cultural center was only useful to the war effort as a temporary transport junction on the imploding Eastern Front. American bombers concentrated on the railroad yards, and the British went after everything else. It was the biggest firestorm since Hamburg. The death toll will never be known, although estimates range from thirty thousand to three hundred thousand. After reducing it to cinder, Harris savagely bombed the city again with explosives, aiming to kill off remaining survivors in the cellars.

Roosevelt's endorsement of Thunderclap, which paved the way for U.S. complicity in Dresden, was a moral watershed in the American conduct of the war. By committing the Air Force to British doctrine in Germany, Thunderclap also opened the door to the Zoroastrian Society alumni, who wanted an unrestricted incendiary campaign against Japan's "paper cities." The hundred thousand or so German civilians whom the Eighth Air Force burned to death in the cities of eastern Germany during the winter of 1945 were but a prelude to the one million Japanese consumed in the B-29 autos-da-fé later that spring.

These ghosts of the Good War's darkest side still haunt the toxic waste surrounding German Village. Now that Potsdamer Platz and the other open wounds of Berlin's history have been transformed into showpieces of reunified prosperity, Mendelsohn's forlorn Mietskasernen suddenly seem significant, as a reproof to the self-righteousness of punishing "bad places" by bombing them. German Village is Berlin's secret heartache, whispering in the contaminated silence of the Utah desert.

4

BERTOLT BRECHT

In 1937, while living in exile in Denmark, Bertolt Brecht published a series of poems under the title *German War Primer* in the Moscow magazine *Das Wort* (*The Word*). These anti-Nazi poems, which presciently warn of a terrible war to come, were the first incarnation of the *War Primer*, a project which would accompany Brecht through the vicissitudes of exile for close to a decade. In early 1940, then living in Sweden, Brecht began cutting out photographs of the rapidly spreading conflict from newspapers and magazines and pasting them into his *Arbeitsjournal*. He had always been fascinated by the potential of photography, and soon was composing four-and eight-line quatrains, most of them rhymed, and transposing them upon the photographs. It was around this time that Brecht began to refer to these montages as his "photo-epigrams."

In the spring of 1941, the Brecht family finally received visas to enter the United States and they left for California via Moscow and Vladivostok only days before Hitler launched a massive German invasion of Soviet Russia. Once in Santa Monica, Brecht actively resumed the project, and by the time the war ended in 1945, he had completed seventy-one photo-epigrams. The poems move quickly from one register and tone to another, from destructive rage and invective to sly wit and sarcasm, from cool detachment to profound sympathy for the victims of the war. One familiar Brechtian technique utilized here is an indirect form of quotation—isolating particular phrases and lines by historical actors such as Hitler and Churchill, and irreverently placing them into carefully manipulated contexts. The epigrams are clearly rhetorical, and often unreservedly didactic, but what they impart is less a systematic doctrine than a way of thinking about human life in its social and historical situation. Here Brecht is wordsmith, instructor, and decoder of ideology in its various forms.

If there is one characteristic of all the poems in the *War Primer*, it is their irrepressibly subversive spirit. It was precisely this quality, however, which made publication of the work problematical. After remaining in the U.S. until 1947, Brecht settled with his wife Helene Weigel in East Berlin. He submitted the *War Primer* to Volk und Welt, a large East German publisher that had expressed interest in the project, but the cultural authorities of the newly founded German Democratic Republic prevented its publication, describing the work as "too broadly pacifist." There were also problems with the collection's aesthetic, which proved difficult to reconcile with the Stalinist doctrine of Socialist Realism. Various changes were demanded, aimed primarily at making the collection more clearly critical of Western capitalism and imperialism, and less "broadly pacifist." But Brecht refused the most crucial of these demands, and the *War Primer* remained unpublished in East Germany until 1955, a decade after the fall of the Third Reich. The work's explicitly anti-capitalist polemics did not make it any more palatable in the West, and a complete edition of the *War Primer* did not appear in Germany until 1994.

Daniel Slager

BRITTISKA BOMBER ÖVER BERLIN

Under sensommaren företog det brittiska flyget åtskilliga raider mot Hamburg, Bremen och andra större tyska städer av industriell eller militär betydelse. Över Berlin fällde britterna för första gången bomber under en nattlig raid den 10—11 september. Bilden visar ett hus i Berlin, som har utsatts för brittisk bombfällning.

Search no longer, woman, you won't see them again!
But it is not Fate, woman, that is to blame.
Those dark forces tormenting your brain,
They each have a face, an address, and a name.

We called ourselves, boasting, sharks of the sky.
Along crowded coastlines we went flying
With gruesome teeth on our sides,
But this time we knew we weren't lying.

The invaders are coming, clear the way!
The city is dead, only rubble remains,
There's never been such order in Roubaix!
It's order that has made the ultimate gains.

10
maj

Gang law is something I understand,
With man-eaters I can deal.
I have the killers eating from my hand,
It's civilization I can heal.

Like a sleepwalker who won't go amiss,
I know the path. Fate prescribes the course it runs.
It's a narrow one that leads to the abyss,
I can find it in my sleep, won't you come?

Her breasts featured in military trim,
With old war medals over her cunt,
Hollywood joins the war against Hitler.
Blood becomes semen. Nervous sweat becomes phlegm.

THE ART
OF SINKING
STIG DAGERMAN

SINK A LITTLE! TRY TO SINK A LITTLE! When it comes to the art of sinking there are worse and better artists. In Germany there are bad practitioners who keep themselves alive only by the thought that since they have so little to live for they have even less to die for. But there are surprisingly many who are willing to accept anything merely to survive.

On Sundays outside the Zoo Station in Berlin a ragged and blind old man sits playing shrill psalm-tunes on a little portable organ. He sits bare-headed in the cold and listens sorrowfully in the direction of his shabby cap down on the pavement, but the German coins make a faint dull clink and only rarely do they fall into the caps of the blind. It would, of course, be a little better for him if he did not play the organ, and above all if he did not play psalms. On weekday afternoons, when the people of Berlin draw past with their small creaking handcarts after yet another day of hunting for potatoes or firewood in the less harrowed suburbs, the blind man has exchanged his harmonium for a barrel organ, and the coins drop more frequently, but on Sunday he insists with quite uneconomic idealism on using his squeaky harmonium. On Sundays he cannot accept his hurdy-gurdy. He still has a little bit further to sink. But in the stations it is possible to meet people who have passed most of the stages. The big German railway stations, once the scene of colorful adventurers strutting their stuff, contain between their scarred walls and beneath their cracked roofs a high percentage of the sum of hopelessness. In rainy weather the stranger is always surprised to see and hear the rain pattering down through the waiting room roof and forming lakes on the floor between the benches. It seems like a tiny revolution in this disciplined chaos. At night the stranger will start as he stumbles against refugees in the concrete tunnels, refugees from the east or from the south, lying stretched out on the naked floor along the naked walls and either sleeping heavily or sitting crouched among their poor bundles and waiting all too wide awake for a train that will take them to a new station, just as hopeless as this one.

The underground stations in the big cities have come through in better shape. They are run-down but unscathed. Berlin's *Untergrundbahnstationen* smell of wetness and poverty, but the trains run promptly as in peacetime. One does not turn to stare at the foreign soldiers walking the platforms with well-dressed but badly made-up German girls who are already speaking perfectly whiny American or quick conciliatory English. Many of these girls stand leaning against the sides of the train doors trying to catch as many eyes as possible with their provocative glances and telling their English soldier that the people here have no sense; others prop up their drunk American friend and make eyes that say: "What can a poor girl do?"

The smoke from their Allied cigarettes blends inside the compartments with the smoke of the German cigarettes, which tastes sour and stifling, and gives the underground trains their persistent smell of dirt and destitution. But when the underground trains come up into the sharp light of day these girls too have faces with the shadows of hunger. And it happens—rarely, no doubt, but it does happen—that someone says: "That's what the future of Germany looks like! A drunk pimply American and a whore of a German girl!"

It happens rarely because sheer necessity wears down the habit of moralizing on behalf of others. It is not true to claim, as a well-fed army chaplain from California said over his steak on the Northern Express, that Germany is a country without morality. It is just that in this country of privation morality has acquired quite a new dimension, whose very existence unaccustomed eyes simply do not notice. This new morality postulates that there are conditions in which it is not immoral to steal, since in these circumstances theft means not depriving someone of his property, but a more just distribution of available goods; likewise, black-marketing and prostitution are not immoral when they have become the only means of survival. This does not mean, of course, that everyone steals, that everyone deals on the black market or goes in for prostitution, but it does mean that, even among certain youthful church groups, people consider that for the sake of endurance it is morally more

reprehensible to starve or let your family starve than to do something that in a normal sense is forbidden. Necessary crime is regarded with more tolerance in Germany than anywhere else; that is one aspect of what the Allied chaplain calls lack of morality. Sinking is more readily forgiven than going under.

One afternoon as darkness is falling and when the power has been cut in Berlin I meet a little Polish schoolteacher in the twilight of a station where the trains to Potsdam rattle past. She has a boy of seven who is taking a childish interest in the remains of a two-year-old train crash out at the edge of the sidings. Passenger coaches with crushed skulls lie tumbled and broken along the side of the rails, a burned-out bogie-car has hurtled into the rusty skeleton of a disintegrated sleeping car, two freight wagons stand defiantly at cross-purposes, and dead limbs of undercarriages stick up out of the fragments.

By the side of the track all the way into Berlin there are old, rusty train wrecks. At each station the platforms are black with people. Crowds with rucksacks, bundles of brushwood, cabbage heads in tattered paper, and little carts all rush in through the doors, and all the time between two stations there is someone or other wailing in pain. Two women screech unceasingly over a trifle. Trampled dogs whimper, but on a bench sit two silent Russian officers surrounded by a little wall of frightened respect.

In short sentences constantly broken off by the crush at new stations or by curses from people whose rucksacks are too big, I slowly find out what it feels like to live in great loneliness in Berlin. The Polish teacher lost her husband in Auschwitz and then she lost two children on the road from the Polish border to Berlin in the big panic in 1945, and the seven-year-old boy is all she has left. Yet she has a calm face when the lights come on, and when I ask her what she busies herself with she whispers with a laugh in my ear: "*Geschäft!*" At one time she read Hamsun and Strindberg in a little Polish village, but "now that's all in the past."

What, though, does she mean by "Geschäft"? We talk a little about longing, since everyone who is forced to remain in Germany longs to be where they are not, unless they are too old to be able to long, or unless they have the desperate courage to believe they have a mission. The Polish teacher longs for Sweden or Norway. She has a picture at home that helps her with her longing. It shows a Norwegian fjord—or the Danube at Siebenbrügen. Would I come home and say which, to save her from longing in the wrong direction?

From the underground station we have many dark streets to negotiate. There has just been an election, and the big posters are still hanging on the walls of the ruins. The Social Democrats: "Where there is fear there is no freedom; without freedom there is no democracy." The Communists: "Youth belongs to us." The Christian Democrats: "Christianity, Socialism, Democracy." The CDU is a chameleon that won in Hamburg thanks to crude anti-Marxist propaganda and tried to win in Berlin through an equally diligent use of the word "socialism."

But what does "Geschäft" in fact mean?

If whispered it means the black market, if said out loud it means business in general. She has a two-room flat at the top of a tenement whose roof has been blasted off. People are already standing waiting on the stairs: someone who wants to get rid of a clock; someone else who has suddenly realized that he needs an Oriental carpet; an old lady, fine as china, who would rather have something to eat instead of her old solid silver service. The doorbell rings all evening and the big room is full of people eagerly muttering about porcelain, clocks, furs, carpets and incredible sums of money. I sit in a small inner room and try to chat with the silent boy who is seven but whose eyes are at least ten years older. The picture shows a completely anonymous landscape. I drink tea with rare white sugar. In a pause the teacher comes in and says she doesn't like all this.

"Once I was so shy I'd hardly open my mouth. Now I spend my days traveling round trying to sniff out people who have gold and silver. You mustn't think I like it. But one has to live here too. And if you want to live you have to get used to everything."

Yes, one must live, and of course one must get used to everything. Her companion, a newly returned soldier, comes in and keeps me company for a time. He was in Italy and has a damaged forehead as a memento of the first Allied landing on Sicily and a grenade splinter in his breast as a souvenir of the siege of Monte Cassino. If he is reproved for being a black-marketeer he says: "I have an allowance of forty-five marks a month. That's enough for seven cigarettes."

When asked if he was a Nazi he replies that he spent seven years in the war and that he takes that to be enough of an answer. When asked if he has voted he says he has, but it won't do any good. And which party? The Christian Democrats? No, he is not religious. The Communists? No, he has friends who were POWs in Russian camps. That leaves the Social Democrats, because they mean the least to him.

But he carries memories not only from Nettuno and Monte Cassino, but also from a Berlin that was once a friendly place. He is able to tell jokes. He tells me the one about the four occupiers of Berlin who rule over a pond where each has his own goldfish. The Russian catches his goldfish and eats it up. The Frenchman catches his and throws it away after pulling off the beautiful fins. The American stuffs his and sends it home to the United States as a souvenir. The Englishman behaves most strangely of all: he catches his fish, holds it in his hand, and caresses it to death.

This freezing, starving, surreptitiously bargaining, dirty and immoral Berlin can still tell funny stories, can still be friendly enough to ask lonely strangers home to tea, still has such people as this Polish teacher and this soldier, who are certainly living unlawfully but who serve, paradoxically enough, as points of light in a great darkness, since they have sufficient courage to sink with their eyes open.

But as I take the odd-smelling underground home in the evening there is a small drunk English soldier-boy sitting between two dissipated blondes whose rigid smiles look as if they belonged to the wrong faces. He caresses both of them, but then, when he leaves the train alone, the smiles quickly drop from the faces, and the two girls set up a raw, humorless wrangle that lasts for over three stations, and the air tingles with hysteria. Nothing could be less like goldfish than those two.

—1946

Translated from the Swedish by Robin Fulton

Under the Rubble III

When I went for water a house fell on me
We bore the house
The forgotten dog and I.
Don't ask me how
I don't remember
Ask the dog how.

★ ★ ★

I left you during the night tonight
For a long time, it seems to me: forever.
The morning was a gray chamber
And as you left there was smoke in the streets.

FROM
SIMPLE STORIES

INGO SCHULZE

BLINKING BABY

Berlin, a Sunday evening in August. Lydia tells about Jenny, Maik, Jan, and Alex, and eats rice pudding. An old man is sitting out on his balcony. There's a signal light on the windowsill. Who and what belongs where.

The rice pudding is still lukewarm when I dish myself a plateful. I make a dent in the middle and fill it with pieces of canned mandarin orange. The juice gathers in a thin circle around the edge of the plate. I sprinkle the pudding with sugar and cinnamon, and hold the spoon almost vertical so that the whole thing doesn't spill over.

The signal light on the windowsill has stopped blinking. It reacts immediately to variations in the light. The glass is yellowish, almost orange, with a metal triangle at the top by which to hang it. The black lettering on the yellow case reads: SIGNALITE.

My kitchen window looks out onto the courtyard. The old man is still sitting out on his balcony in the ell to my left. He suns himself in the afternoon. Usually he listens to Mozart and Wagner and other pieces that sound familiar, although I don't really know what they are. When he opens his balcony door, what I see first are the trembling fingers of his left hand, which he uses to steady himself on the frame. He supports himself with a cane in his right hand. His feet and calves are swollen and purplish.

He walks as if he were wearing incredibly heavy boots in which he had to check at every step to see if the floor will hold. It takes a long time before he sits down, his hands clutching the handle of the cane, one atop the other, or each pressed to a thigh. About every half hour he slides his chair a little to continue facing the sun. By four o'clock he's turned around directly toward me. He wears white underpants, a bathrobe, and sunglasses. He's balding, but a few strands of hair fall down over his collar. He apparently fell asleep during the oboe concerto. It's almost six o'clock in the evening now.

This heat leaves me exhausted. I lie awake at night. It doesn't even help if there's a draft. This morning two guys were kicking a tin can back and forth, right outside our building. That was about five o'clock. Then some crows started carrying on a conversation. I swear they were talking about something. And finally, a telephone rang somewhere close by; all the windows are wide open. Just when I finally fell asleep, Jan was at the door. He'd come directly from Tresor Disco. The toilet attendants and bouncers wanted to go home, and there was no second shift because of vacations. So they had to close down early. Jan wanted to show me the signal light he and Alex had stolen from a construction site on Botzow Strasse. They'd been hopping around in their disco bunker all night, waving this signal light. What happened then I'm not sure. Jan just said that it was all over between him and Alex, the end, over and done with, and finally asked if he could move in with me for just a few days. But I'm not going to let him even get to square one with that.

Then, around eleven, Jenny and Maik came by. France didn't last a week.

Maik's left hand was bandaged up in a sling. I keep their keys. They share a two-and-a-half room apartment with Alex and Jan one floor down.

Jenny came back alone later in the afternoon. She took off again a half hour ago, and I don't know if I should be angry or hurt, or just take it all as a sign of helplessness, maybe even of trust. There was a time when I would've laughed it off. Of course I'm glad she came to see me. I could be her mother, theoretically speaking.

At times we're a kind of family. They don't even notice when they're starting to get on my nerves. They think they have to look after me because I'm lonely. They placed a personal ad for me in Zitty. And ever since they saw some of Patrick's photographs lying around in the apartment, they've wanted me to write to him. I've told them several times that Patrick was the reason I had to get out of Altenburg. That night with the Holitzschek woman was the last straw. Her and her not-so-secret secret. Besides, as I always say, getting out of there was just the first step toward putting some order back in my life. And I'm not about to let that order fly out the window, even if Jenny and the three guys do carry on as if being alone were the worst thing ever. I always thought it was completely different for young kids. Plus the fact—which they don't even take into account—that Patrick has found a new girlfriend and a new job.

Jenny was hungry at any rate. She opened the fridge and shouted, "When are you ever going to eat all this?" Her hand was resting on the shelf she was checking out.

"I can warm up the lasagna," I said. "There's veggie lasagna left over from lunch."

She took a package of nasi-goreng from the freezer and turned it over a few times until she found the cooking instructions. The pastel blue sleeveless blouse I gave her is too big for her. "You can do it in a pan, too," Jenny said. "Want some?"

"Why not the veggie lasagna?" I asked.

Then Jenny held up a can. "Mandarin oranges! Can I open it? There's still one left."

She shoved the nasi-goreng back into the freezer. "My mother never puts cans in the fridge, uses too much electricity," she said, bending down and pulling out a jelly jar to see what was behind it.

"Mmmm, rice pudding!" She held up a package of Ravensberg Rice Pudding with both hands. "Lyyyydia—please, please, please, please!" The vegetable bin was sticking out and the fridge door wouldn't close.

"Have you got cinnamon, sugar and cinnamon?" she asked.

"Jenny," I said, "the fridge." She forced the door shut, grabbed a paring knife from the drawer, sawed along the dotted line of the rice pudding package, and tore off the tip.

"Where's the garbage can?" she asked. I showed her the bag for recycled paper under the sink. The next thing she shouted was, "Yuck, look at this apple!" It had a big brown spot.

Jenny turned over the other apples and grapefruits in the straw basket. "This's the only one," she said, halving it with the bread knife. "This got its own place, too?" I showed her the green tub for biodegradables, and told her about Jan and Alex and the signal light.

"When you're still flying and they close down, it's like having your heart give out," Jenny explained to me. She meant dancing and the stuff they swallow to get high. "That light really bugs me," she said. "What a stupid gizmo. Even when I can't see it, I can feel it. Why'd they bring something like that home? It really gets to me."

"Jan says it's his baby now," I said. "At least for as long as he's alone."

"Great! His baby, not mine," she said. "First of all, he's already in the sack with Alex again, and second they wouldn't let me keep the cat, either. Baby!" she shouted. "Another baby! That gizmo starts blinking whenever it gets a little darker. It really bugs me." She diced the apple. You could see a white stripe where her blouse had slipped off her tanned right shoulder.

I asked about Maik's hand. Jenny sniffed. "He's packing his stuff right now. I told him to pack. Can I turn this on?" She fidgeted with the radio dials. "First he says I shouldn't worry about money, and five days later he's broke. I was furious, nothing but restaurants and bars. What station is that? I wanted to see Paris! Instead we spent two days hanging around cemeteries in Reims. Now he's acting as if I ran through all his money." She turned the radio off again. "Maik got caught in the middle somewhere, two guys were arguing, and airhead that he is, Mr. Bigshot stuck his hand in between." Jenny had opened the oven and pulled out the skillets. "There was this really nice guy who'd given us a ride," she said. "Maik wanted to go to Stuttgart, to see his parents. I said, no problem, go ahead, but count me out. I said not in a truck, but Maik asked the driver anyway. It had 'Berlin' written on it, but the driver was headed for Meerane, wherever that is. A Volvo rig full of Spanish oranges he'd picked up in France. Eddie, the driver, talked the whole time. If he stopped talking, he said, he'd fall asleep. We were supposed to entertain him, fifty jokes before we got to the Hermsdorf interchange. That pissed Maik off, and he told the driver to turn on the radio instead. Well, you know," Jenny said, setting the medium-sized skillet on the stove. "At the Kirchheim interchange Eddie said he wanted to pay for our dinner and a night in a motel. That was okay by me, paying the way for two people who're broke. I'd already told him the story about the lifeguard. We understood each other."

I didn't know what she was talking about.

"Come on," she said, "I know you know the swimming pool story."

"No, I don't," I said.

"Easy to see how well you listen," Jenny said and held the spark lighter to the burner.

"That was the day before I got my first ID card. In April of '89. I was at an indoor pool with a girlfriend. We wanted to jump in, but this woman lifeguard demanded we put our clothes back on and leave, because some training session was about to start. I got out my watch—there was at least another twenty minutes to go." Jenny put butter in the skillet, bent down, and turned up the heat.

"You'd just been messing around till then?"

"We'd paid. Besides, there was still time left. We had our bathing caps on. Suddenly a whole pack of competition swimmers—that's what they called them—stormed in. They started played dodge ball with us, pushing us around in a circle. I just kept thinking, don't cry, don't cry. Nobody gave a shit about us. But we jumped into the water anyway, with our knees all scraped up. When we turned in our locker keys at the entrance, that same lifeguard was sitting at the desk. She even said 'Thank you.'" Jenny swirled the melted butter around in the skillet. "And for the first time in my life I'd seen what grown-ups are really like, and how you're treated when higher-ups can get back at you without ever getting their hands dirty. I was going to tell my mother about it that night. But once she was standing there beside my bed, I knew I couldn't say anything about it. It would've been worse for her than it'd been for me. I couldn't do that to her."

Jenny tossed the diced apple into the skillet. She'd slipped out of her run-down sandals as she moved about, and now she used her toes to pull my scale out from beneath the cabinets, stood on it, stepped off, and tried a second time.

"Look at that," she cried. "That can't be. A hundred and eleven. I don't even weigh a hundred!" Her shoulder blades stood out like two wings. "A hundred and eleven! Have a look for yourself!" She got out of the way to let me try and watched the pointer.

"A hundred and fifty," I said. "Works fine."

"What? You weigh a hundred and fifty?" Jenny looked me up and down.

I shoved the scale back under the shelving and asked again about Maik's hand.

"I couldn't really tell the lifeguard story, because Maik was constantly interrupting," Jenny said, stepping over her sandals to put a bowl and some cinnamon on the table, shoving the sugar bowl toward me. "He kept honing in," she said, "until Eddie asked him to please leave me alone and let me talk. And when that didn't help he yelled at Maik to shut his trap. Eddie was right, Lydie, he really was." Jenny glanced over at me. I told her to use a wooden spoon instead of a fork, and to turn down the heat.

"So when Maik and I were alone in the motel room—Eddie was still sitting in the restaurant—Maik starts in on me. Why had I told Eddie that story when I'd never told it to him before? Imagine anybody coming at you with something like that—but it's typical Maik. Besides, he pisses in the shower."

"All men do," I said.

"Maik started talking bullshit. He wouldn't stand in my way if I wanted to earn a little extra tonight—that's the kind of crap he was giving me. Well that did it for me," Jenny cried. "I'd told him one time," she said, "about a guy I'd gotten together with occasionally, before Maik and I were an item. He was a lot older, but OK, very polite and generous, and absolutely nuts about me. Everything I did drove him wild. He was always slipping me a little money, instead of presents. But for some reason he couldn't get it on. I figured maybe it was paternal, an instinct to protect me or whatever. But then out of the blue he read me this filthy story, a kind of s&m thing that would've been totally absurd if it hadn't been him. And so everything just fell apart for me, the whole image I had of him. And I told Maik about it, which was way unnecessary. And ever since then he thinks I'm hiding things from him, some s&m rough stuff or whatever's going on inside that wacko brain of his. Just because the guy gave me some money. But that's Maik all over. It wasn't till they brought him back that I realized he'd locked me in the room. One of the waitresses drove us to the hospital and back. Meanwhile, the other one had found a guy who'd take us to Berlin. He dropped us off at Wannsee station, and didn't say a single word the whole way."

I told her she should wear something under the blouse, because otherwise just one little gesture and you could see everything.

"Not there," I said when Jenny pressed her chin to her chest. "Here, at the sleeves."

"A little unappetizing?" she asked. "They kind of stick out sideways—repulsive, huh?" Suddenly she threw her arms around my neck. I just had time to get to my feet. I held Jenny tight and stroked her hair. My left shoulder felt wet. That's how I knew she was crying. But then, just as abruptly as she had thrown herself at me, she pulled away.

I mixed the sugar and cinnamon, set the table for two, and asked if she'd like anything to drink.

"Same as you," Jenny said, stirring the rice pudding into the diced apples. She tore the package all the way open. "Serve chilled, with muesli," she read, and turned the heat up again. The can of mandarin oranges in her hand, she started looking for an opener. The rice pudding began bubbling at the edges. "Could you?" she asked, handing me the can and the opener, and stirred the mixture.

Suddenly Jenny said, "You're probably right, maybe being alone is best."

Just as I got the can open, the doorbell rang. "It's for you," I said, and didn't stand up until it rang a second time.

So Jenny left. I heard her open the door. But she didn't say anything. Then the door closed. I waited. I called her name and finally went to find her. I was alone.

I took the rice pudding off the stove, then stood awhile at the apartment door and waited. There was no one in the stairwell, either. I turned the burner off and ran myself a bath. That always helps. Sitting in the tub, I played with an empty shampoo bottle. I picked it up with my feet and set it on the bathtub rim, concentrated, and just nudged it with my toes so that it fell back into the water. It's like playing billiards, and it's good for the stomach muscles, too.

When the doorbell rang again, I ran to the door in my bathrobe. There on my doormat was the signal light, blinking away. I bent down over the banister—nothing. I took the signal light back to the kitchen and set it on the windowsill, where it immediately stopped blinking.

I eat the whole plateful, but still don't know what to think about this stunt. I dish up the rest of the rice pudding. First I wash the skillet, which only fits at an angle partway in the sink. Then I fill the empty pudding package with water so it'll be easier to rinse later.

Then I eat some more.

There are no sounds coming from either the courtyard or the apartment below. If those four were my kids, I'd blame myself and feel guilty that they're so rude, so chaotic.

Or I'd convince myself that it was the bad neighborhood or hard times somehow, or the heat

The old man is still sleeping. When he wakes up he'll wonder where the day has gone. A perfect excuse. But he probably doesn't need excuses anymore. Last spring, he always left green bananas on his balcony. He used the crook of his cane to pull them over, feel them, and then shove them away again. One corner of his bathrobe would dangle back and forth. His joints are going to hurt. I can't even sleep in a bed, and the old man can take his catnap right there on a chair like that. He'll probably feel it worst in his neck and shoulders, and tonight he'll lie awake just like me, listening to music, wondering about the blinking light, asking himself what it means. Maybe it could have a soothing effect, though. If you closed your eyes it might have a soothing effect, sort of like the ticking of the alarm clock I used to have. I was eleven and twelve and thirteen and never told my mother, not just because I was afraid, but because I thought it would be worse for her than for me, and I couldn't do that to her. But then she divorced the man who fathered me, divorced him for completely different reasons.

Once I've finished all the pudding, I'll rinse the plate and the rice pudding package. Maybe it'd be better if I put the SIGNALITE in the wardrobe, under my winter things, or in the bathroom with the light on. Tomorrow morning I have to take the recyclable paper down. They empty the yellow cans on Mondays. I'll put Jenny's sandals on her doormat and set the SIGNALITE beside them. And if Jan doesn't want his baby anymore, now that Alex is back, then he'll just have to return it to the construction site on Botzow Strasse. That would be the perfect solution, and everything would be in its place again.

FISH

Jenny tells about a new job and Martin Meurer. The boss shows them the ropes. Where is the North Sea? At first everything goes well. Then Jenny has to do a bit of interpreting. What happened to the fish during Noah's Flood? Topped off with a brass band.

He's standing between two chairs, wearing green gym shorts and trying to climb into a diving suit, the one with red stripes that I tried on yesterday. The one with blue stripes is lying on the table. We shake hands. He says, "Martin Meurer," and I say, "Jenny."

"The other one is even smaller," he says, "but the flippers are good." I turn my back to him and undress. And pop a button off my jacket. I get into the blue-striped diving suit and tug the hood up over my head. You can't see my hair or my ears or my neck. It makes my face look almost chubby. I pack up my things and wait until he gets his flippers on.

He's holding a plastic bag in his right hand, diving goggles and a snorkel in his left, and walks as carefully as a stork down the hall toward Kerndel's— the restaurant manager's—office. He knocks twice. I tell him to open the door. We sit down in the two chairs along the wall to our left and wait.

"I look like a nun," I say.

"No," he says. "Like some reporter playing astronaut. You ever done it before?"

"What?" I ask.

"This. You got into your gear so fast."

"I was here yesterday," I say, "but they won't let you do it alone."

"It's pretty warm in these suits," he says.

"My feet are cold," I say.

"My feet are cold too," he says. "But the rest of me . . ."

"Hello, Jenny!" Kerndel exclaims "Well, how's it going?"

We stand up. "Meurer," he says, introducing himself as he clutches the plastic bag between his knees. "Martin Meurer."

Kerndel puts out his hand. We sit back down. Kerndel leans against the desk, picks up a piece of paper, and turns it over. He goes through the same routine as yesterday. "And then you ask your questions: 'Where is the North Sea?' Or, 'Can you tell us where we can find the North Sea around here?' Or, 'How do I get to the North Sea?' However you want to put it, but North Sea has to be in there, got it?" he says.

"Yes," I say, "no problem."

Kemdel looks at him. "Got it?"

"Got it," Martin replies, lifting his right flipper and slapping it on the carpet.

"And always be cheerful and spread good cheer," I say.

"You bet!" Kerndel says. "Otherwise you two can just stay at home." He slides a little farther along the edge of the desk and stares at his own pale hand rubbing the piece of paper up and down his thigh like a washrag. The paper looks like a large ticket, part of which can be torn off along a perforated line ("Tear Here—Keep in Your Wallet"); the other part is a map of the city. Stylized red fish mark the locations of the various branches of the North Sea restaurant chain. The largest part of the map, however, shows a photograph of the tan, wind-rippled dunes of a desert, above which white letters set against a bluish purple sky read: "Where is the North Sea?"

"And what if they say 'no'?" Kerndel asks.

"'But we do,'" I say. "'Schul Strasse 10a and Schul Strasse 15! You're invited to a fish dinner. It's our May special.' And then we hand them the piece of paper."

"The flyer," Kerndel says, correcting me. "And what if they say 'yes'?" Kerndel looks at Martin.

"How do we get there?" Martin says, and slaps his flipper again.

"Jenny?" Kerndel says "What if they say 'yes'?"

"Great! Take us there?" I say.

"You got all that now?"

Kerndel stares at Martin until he says "Yes." Then Kerndel has him repeat the May special: "Baked plaice with tartar sauce, parsley potatoes, mixed salad, and a point-three liter Coca-Cola. Regular 15.40, now only 12.95."

"It's all here on the flyer," Kernel says. "But don't read from it. That's tacky. There'll be no reading. Now, once more, Jenny."

"Baked plaice with tartar sauce, parsley potatoes, green salsa, plus a large Coke, only 12.95," I say.

"Regular 15.40," Kerndel adds. "Mixed salad and Coca-Cola, point three liters. Put your goggles on. Now talk. Let's hear it, come on . . ."

"How do I get to the North Sea?" I ask. "Do you know where the North Sea is?" Kerndel points to Martin.

"Which way to the North Sea? I want to get to the North Sea! The Sea's the place for me to be! Can you help me out?" Martin says.

"Too nasal, both too nasal, better without goggles," he says. "No, don't take them off. Put them on your forehead. Push the goggles up." The telephone rings, but then stops after the second ring. "And put this like this." Kerndel has stood up and is tugging Martin's snorkel lower. "A little more. That's it! And never too many flyers in your hand at once, four or five at the most, no doubling up, okay? All right?"

We nod.

"So what happened to the fish during Noah's Flood?" Kerndel asks and claps his hands. He puts an arm around my shoulder and pulls me to him, "Now go get 'em." He walks around his desk and picks up the receiver. "It'll be a snap!"

We leave our bags in the secretary's closet, and she gives us blue shoulder bags filled with flyers.

"Can you manage these?" she asks. "A thousand in each." She holds the door open for us. "Just follow this hallway."

Martin stops outside the back door, looks at me, and says, "We've got to go for 'em all—every man and every women—right from the start. Otherwise we get nowhere. If we cop out even once . . ."

I wonder if maybe he was a teacher at one time. I haven't even got the door closed, and he's off and running. Two boys, fourteen or fifteen years old at most, stare at him. "Well, can't you figure it out?" he asks. They give our flippers and shoulder bags the once-over.

"We want to get to the North Sea," I say. They shake their heads.

"Please. The Sea's the place for you and me," he says. "Well, go see for yourselves." Finally they take the flyers.

We head for the pedestrian zone. I say, "Let's leave out kids like them." "Puberty," he says and nods.

And it really goes well. We get into it quick. Usually I start, then he chimes in, "Right, we want to get to the North Sea."

"That's it, the North Sea," I say then, or, "You really don't know where it is?" And then he says, "We'll let you in on a little secret." After a short pause we finish by reciting the address together. People laugh and take the flyers without the least hesitation.

"I'm sorry," Martin says suddenly. "That was stupid of me." I don't know what he's talking about. "Wishing that last bunch 'bon appétit.'"

I tell him I don't think it's such a bad idea, and so when it's my turn for the flyer I add "bon appétit" too. Some people respond with "thanks," or "same to you."

"They're really curious, they actually want us to speak to them," Martin says. "Not shy at all."

If there are a couple of people standing around us, others come over on their own. There's even a little jostling, and we pass out flyers only to people who put out a hand.

"Wonder if he's having us watched?" I ask softly.

"Sure," Martin says. "I tried to sound as natural as you, but he wasn't convinced."

"You kept playing with your flipper," I say.

"What?"

"You wouldn't stop slapping your flipper, like this." And I do it for him. "Didn't you notice?"

He shook his head. "Maybe that's why he was like that."

"He's like that, period," I say. "Nothing you can do about it."

A brass band is playing outside where the pedestrian zone crosses Schloss Platz, near a white tent that comes to a high point. It looks oriental. Next to it is a man being interviewed for television. He has a round yellow sticker on his blue jacket. It reads: "Our Beef—As Safe as It Is Tasty!" The musicians are wearing the same sticker, as are the group of women who are busy grilling steaks and sausages. I now notice people all around me wearing this beef sticker. They're distributing flyers that are larger than ours.

"Would you work for them?" he asks.

"Sure," I say. "Do you think what we're offering is so great?"

"I don't know," he says. "The fish in the picture looks like it's been breaded to death, probably hard as a rock, and it's only .45 cheaper. Think it'll sell?"

When I ask him where he's from, Martin just says, "From the East, from Thuringia." He's visiting his mother here in Stuttgart.

"Kerndel," he says, "didn't mention a word about the pay, the hundred and twenty a day."

"They've got to make good on that," I say. "It's what the ad said."

He nods. Suddenly he says, "One flyer would work for a whole family." My first thought is that he's trying to be witty.

"And for friends and acquaintances," I respond.

"That's true too. If I keep going at this rate, we'll be done by early afternoon."

We still have to distribute flyers near the shops in the pedestrian zone, but even when we don't approach people they stop and stick out a hand. The band keeps playing without a break.

"You mentioned that thing with the flipper," he says.

"And?"

"Do you know that you never stop smiling?"

"You don't either," I say.

About an hour later it starts to drizzle. Most people stay close to the store windows, moving along under the awnings, from overhang to overhang. I step into the shops while Martin goes on working outside. A woman waves to me and calls out, "Hi there, Froggy." I don't interrupt conversations. But when they see me or turn around to look at me, I pretend I'm lost and softly ask, "Excuse me, but do you know where the North Sea might be?" They're shocked for a moment. But once they start laughing I hand them the flyer.

When I don't see Martin outside the window, I go back out. I retrace our steps a bit, but can't find him. There are North Sea flyers lying everywhere. He's sitting with his back to a flagpole and doesn't answer me. His left eye is swollen. He glances up briefly and asks if I've seen his snorkel lying around anywhere. I try to collect a few of Kerndel's flyers, but they're stuck to the wet pavement, and every time I try to bend down to pick one up I step on it with my flippers.

"They give you a hard time, too?" Martin asks when I'm standing in front of him again.

"No," I say, "why?"

"The way you're looking at me."

"That's quite a shiner," I say.

"Have you seen my snorkel?"

I go on looking for a while. All I find is a few more flyers, then I go back to him.

"Sorry," he says, lifting up his snorkel and tapping the mouthpiece against his left flipper. "Was under my flipper, didn't even notice."

"Should I get you some ice?"

"You know what kept running through my mind? That thing about the fish and Noah. I was paralyzed, totally paralyzed," he says. "First the guy looked down, then he glared at me and asked his wife if she knew me. I was standing on his shoes with the tips of my flippers, just a little. I didn't even feel it, and he can't have felt it, either. His wife said she didn't know me. I think he might've even lifted me off the ground a little."

"Are you sick to your stomach?"

"That thing about Noah is so goddam stupid," he says. "I didn't say anything different than usual. Just the same as always."

"We've got to go see Kerndel," I say. "For the insurance. This is an accident."

"I'm not going back there." He slapped the pavement with his flipper.

"I know why it happened," I say, and wait for him to look at me.

"He didn't like the sound of my accent."

"He asked his wife if she knew you, right. And when you said no, he punched you, right?"

"How could I possibly know her? This is the first time I've even been in Stuttgart."

"He was trying to find out if this was a setup," I say. "That's why." Martin doesn't get it. "He figured it might be a big-time setup job, with a hidden camera, or that you might be somebody who'd lost a bar bet," I explain. "Nobody else'd be doing it, nobody your age. The guy thought you were trying to jerk him around. That's all."

He looks at me as if I'd slapped him in the face.

"Not that it's true, of course," I say. "I just mean, that's what that idiot must've been thinking. You're really good, you've got a way of making people happy. You really do spread good cheer, not just these scraps of paper. I'd like to see anybody do it better. Besides, you're in great shape."

He spits between his flippers.

"You made everybody feel good," I say. "We ought to get a lot more money, and not just from Kerndel, but from the mayor—even from insurance companies—for making people feel better."

Martin looks at me. His left eye is swollen shut now.

"The guy's an asshole, the kind that doesn't believe it's possible for someone just to be nice," I say.

"No one bothered to help," he says and spits again. "Nobody budged."

"That's asking too much of them," I say. "People didn't know what they were supposed to make of it, they had no idea what was going on. They'd never seen anything like it. In the middle of the pedestrian zone they see a frogman get punched out. Maybe they thought it doesn't hurt when you're wrapped up in rubber, or that it was part of the act. They didn't want to make asses of themselves if it turned out to be performance art or street theater."

I tell Martin about the old man who died on his balcony in our back courtyard, the guy with the bananas and the loud music. We all thought he was sleeping. And he sat out there in the rain, all night.

"All night?"

"Yes," I say. "It was too dark to see. It wasn't until morning that we noticed him still sitting there. . . . Come on, we're gonna go see Kerndel."

Martin closes his eyes, just like I once saw a woman do in the subway. She just calmly closed her eyes and didn't move a muscle till the doors opened. Martin shakes his head.

"Yes we are," I say, "we've got to."

Translated from the German by John Woods

5

KRISTINA SOLOMOUKHA

SABINE HORNIG

MARIA EICHHORN

MONICA BONVICINI

Monica Bonvicini, Maria Eichhorn, Sabine Hornig, and Kristina Solomoukha are four artists whose work aims to destabilize the social and psychological structures that have emerged alongside Berlin's newly erected architecture. Monica Bonvicini's *Letzter Blick (Last Glimpse)*, created for the first Berlin Biennial in 1998, is a huge pane of glass (98 1/2 x 59 in.) set into the wall of Kunst-Werke, an exhibition space and artists' residency. Bonvicini's work refers to Beatriz Colomina's essay, "The Split Wall: Domestic Voyeurism." According to Colomina, domestic interiors designed by modernist architects Adolf Loos and Le Corbusier defined the sexual hierarchies of interior and exterior spaces; windows were designed not for looking out, but to display the woman within. In contrast, Bonvicini's *Letzter Blick* offers an open view to the outside through which she can enjoy a privileged view of the construction site below.

For the exhibition *On Talking a Normal Situation* in Antwerp's Museum van Hedendaagse Kunst, Maria Eichhorn contracted several building specialists to complete the various stages of her installation sculpture, *French Window*. A Belgian construction company cut into the second floor fire wall of the museum and built a cement beam support for the emerging balcony structure. Using drawings made by an architect, a craftsperson made the door and balcony, which are painted dark blue. The Museum van Hedendaagse Kunst has few windows, and Eichhorn's balcony offered an open view of the docks and ships traveling along the channel to Antwerp's port. The door was left open throughout the exhibition (except during periods of rain and snow), and was removed when the exhibition ended. Like the discoloration exposed when a painting is removed from the wall, *French*

Window remains present, albeit with no measurable trace. Certainly it inspired viewers (particularly the museum staff) to attempt a glimpse of the waterfront even after the door had been replaced by a plain white exhibition wall. And from outside, the local public can no longer peer into the museum. Eichhorn's project demonstrates that a scupture can endure in the mind even when it ceases to exist as matter.

Sabine Hornig's *Twins* is an installation sculpture consisting of two adjacent and nearly identical rooms configured around a central wall, which frames a picture window. On one side, a large-format photographic slide reflects an image of houses taken from the window of an empty storefront in Berlin. When viewed from "outside" the room's window the slide image adds depth and detail to the interior empty space. From "inside" this reversed image seems to be projected onto the opposite gallery wall. Though *Twins* conflicts with the architectural conditions of its exhibition space, it interferes most critically with the supporting preconditions of the imagination.

Kristina Solomoukha often works in the subtler and more traditional mediums of watercolor or small-scale found object sculptures. In a watercolor titled *Fond de Tiroir*, two classic 1950's style desks stand side by side with highways passing through the top drawers and encircling the dual structure. This configuration suggests that at the bottom of it all are two predominant structures: freeways and marriage. In French, *fond de tiroir* implies what is "out of sight and out of mind." Solomoukha's poetic use of language, together with the playful empathy in her work, erect a critique of architecture equal in magnitude to that of Bonvicini, Eichhorn, and Hornig, who use large-scale materials to create their installations.

Cay-Sophie Rabinowitz

Kristina Solomoukha, *Projet (Project)*, 1997–1999.

ABOVE:
Sabine Hornig, *Twins*, Nexus Contemporary Art
Center, Atlanta, 1999.

RIGHT:
Maria Eichhorn, *Wand ohne Bild (Wall without Picture)*,
Martin-Gropius-Bau, Berlin, 1991.

PAGE 136:
Monica Bonvicini, *Letzter Blick (Last Glimpse)*,
Kunst-Werke, Berlin, 1998.

PAGE 137:
Maria Eichhorn, *French Window*, MUHKA,
Antwerp, 1993.

OSKAR PASTIOR

today's arithmetic

at ten I was ten
at twenty around thirty
at thirty barely twenty

forty was forty but not in years
fifty was sixty minus ten
sixty was fifty plus ten

when my mother was born my father turned
nine
when my mother was forty I was half that

when I died I was over sixty
when I was over sixty my father was over thirty
and my mother over three

when I could do sums I was under ten
when I was under ten I was born

Translated from the German by Peter Constantine

A SUMMER HOUSE, LATER

JUDITH HERMANN

STEIN FOUND THE HOUSE DURING THE WINTER. He phoned me sometime early in December and said, "Hello," and then nothing. I didn't say anything either.

He said, "This is Stein."

I said, "I know."

He said, "So, how's it going?"

I said, "Why are you calling?"

He said, "I've found it."

Not understanding, I asked him, "What did you find?" and he answered irritably, "The house! I found the house."

The house. I remembered: Stein and his talk about a house, far from Berlin. A country house, a manor house, linden trees out front, horse chestnuts in the back, a Brandenburg lake, at least two and a half acres of land; maps spread out, marked up, him driving around for weeks in the area, searching. When he came back he looked peculiar, and the others said, "What's he talking about? Nothing's ever going to come of it." I forgot about it afterward, when I didn't see Stein for some time. Just as I forgot about him.

As always when Stein surfaced and I couldn't think of much to say, I automatically lit a cigarette. I said hesitantly, "Stein? Did you buy it?" and he shouted, "Yes!" and then he dropped the telephone. I had never heard him shout before. And then he was back on the line and shouting, "You have to see it, it's incredible, it's great!" I didn't ask why I, of all people, ought to look at it. For a long time he said nothing more.

"What are you doing right now?" he finally asked. It sounded downright obscene, and his voice trembled slightly. "Nothing," I said. "I'm just sitting around and reading the paper."

"I'll pick you up. In ten minutes," Stein said and hung up.

Five minutes later he was at my house. He didn't take his thumb off the doorbell until long after I had opened the door. I said, "Stein, this is getting on my nerves. Stop ringing." I wanted to say, "Stein, it's freezing outside, I don't feel like driving out there with you, get lost." He stopped ringing the bell, tilted his head as if he wanted to say something, but said nothing. I got dressed. We drove off. His taxi smelled of cigarettes, so I rolled down the window and turned my face toward the cold air.

My relationship with Stein, as the others referred to it, had been over for two years. It hadn't lasted long, and consisted mainly of trips we took together in his taxi, which was where I had first met him. He was driving me to a party, and on the autobahn he pushed a Trans Am cassette into the tape player; when we got to the party I said it must be somewhere else and we drove on, and at some point he switched off the meter. He came home with me. He put his plastic bags down in the hallway and stayed for three weeks. Stein had never had an apartment of his own; he moved around the city with these bags and slept here and there, and when he couldn't find anywhere to go he slept in his taxi. He wasn't what one thinks of as a homeless person. He was clean, well-dressed, never seedy. He had money because he was working, but he didn't have his own apartment. Maybe he didn't want one.

During the three weeks that Stein lived at my place, we drove all over the city in his taxi. The first time we went out together we drove down Frankfurter Allee to where it ends and back again, listening to Massive Attack, smoking and driving up and down for probably an hour until Stein said, "Do you understand?" My head was completely empty, I felt hollowed out and in a strange state of suspended animation. The street before us was broad and wet from the rain, the wipers moved across the windshield, back and forth. The Stalin-era buildings on both sides of the street were huge and strange and beautiful. The city was no longer the city I knew, it was autarkical and deserted. Stein said, "Like a giant prehistoric animal." I said I understood: I had stopped thinking.

For every route Stein had a different kind of music: Ween for country roads, David Bowie for downtown, Bach for the avenues, Trans Am only for the autobahn. We almost always drove on the autobahn. When the first snow fell, Stein got out of the car at every rest area, ran to a snow-covered field, and performed slow and concentrated Tae Kwon Do movements until, laughing and furious, I shouted to him to come back, I wanted to drive on, I was cold.

At some point I had had enough. I packed up his three plastic bags and said it was time for him to find a new place to stay. He thanked me and left. He moved in with Christiane, who lived on the floor below me, then with Anna, with Henrietta, with Falk, and then with the others. He screwed them all, that was unavoidable; he was pretty good-looking, Fassbinder would have been delighted with him. He was there with us, and yet also not there. He didn't belong, but for one reason or another he stayed. He posed as a model in Falk's studio, laid cable for Anna's concerts, and went to Heinze's readings at the Red Salon. He applauded when we applauded in the theater, drank when we drank, took drugs when we took them. He came with us to parties, and in the summer he came along when we drove out to the shabby, lopsided little country houses, on one of whose rotting fences someone had scrawled *Berliner raus!* And now and then one of us would take him to bed, and now and then one of us watched.

Not me. I didn't repeat. Frankly, it wasn't my kind of thing. Nor could I remember what it was like—that is, what sex with Stein had been like.

We sat around with him, in the gardens and houses of people we had nothing to do with. Workers had lived there, small farmers, and amateur gardeners who hated us and whom we hated. We avoided the locals, just thinking of them ruined everything. It wasn't right. We robbed them of the sense they had of being among themselves, we disfigured their villages, their fields, and even their sky, the way we strode around with our *Easy Rider* gait, flicking our burnt-down roaches into the flower beds in their front yards, the way we nudged each other excitedly. But we wanted to be there regardless. Inside the houses we tore down wallpaper, removed rubber and plastic. Stein did that. We sat in the garden, drank wine, gazed idiotically at "Tree Clump Circled by Swarm of Gnats," and talked about Castorf and Heiner Müller, and Wawerzinek's latest flop at the Volksbühne. When Stein had finished, he sat down with us. He had nothing to say. We took LSD, Stein took it too. Toddi staggered into the evening light, driveling something about "blue" every time she touched anything, while Stein smiled with exaggerated cheerfulness and said nothing. He couldn't get the knack of our sophisticated, neurasthenic, fucked-up ways, although he tried; mostly he looked at us as though we were actors performing on a stage. Once I was alone with him—maybe it was in the garden of Heinze's house in Lunow, the others having set off for the sunset, on speed. Stein was putting away glasses, ashtrays, bottles, and chairs. Soon there was nothing left to remind us of the others. "Do you want some wine?" he asked. I said, "Yes," we drank, smoked in silence, and he smiled every time our eyes met. That was it.

I thought, "And that was it," as I sat now next to Stein in the taxi, on Frankfurter Allee, heading toward Prenzlau in the afternoon traffic. The day was hazy and cold, dust in the air, goggle-eyed, stupid, tired drivers next to us, giving us the finger. I smoked a cigarette and wondered why I was sitting next to Stein now, why of all people he had called me —was it because I had been a beginning for him? Because he couldn't reach Anna or Christiane or Toddi? Because none of them would have driven out there with him? And why was I driving out there with him? I couldn't get close to an answer. I threw the cigarette butt out the window, ignoring the comments of the driver next to us. It was awfully cold in the taxi. "Is something wrong with the heater, Stein?" Stein didn't answer. It was the first time just the two of us were sitting in his car again since then. Indulgently I said, "Stein, what kind of house is it? What did you pay for it?"

Stein looked absentmindedly into the rearview mirror, drove through a red light, changed lanes, drew on his cigarette till the glowing end reached his lips. He said, "80,000. I paid 80,000 marks for it. It's beautiful. I saw it and I knew—this is it." He had red spots on his face and pounded on the horn with the flat of his hand as he pulled ahead of a bus that had the right of way. I said, "Where did you get 80,000 marks?" He glanced at me briefly and answered, "You're asking the wrong questions." I decided not to say any more.

We left Berlin. Stein got off the autobahn, turned onto a country road, and it began to snow. I felt tired, as I always do riding in cars. I stared at the windshield wipers, into the whirling snow coming toward us in concentric circles, I thought about driving with Stein two years ago, about the odd euphoria, about the indifference, about the strangeness. Stein was driving more calmly, glancing at me now and then. I asked, "Doesn't the tape deck work anymore?" He smiled, said, "Oh sure. I didn't know . . . whether you still like it." I rolled my eyes, "Of course I do," and pushed the Callas cassette —the one on which Stein had recorded a Donizetti aria twenty times in succession—into the tape deck. He laughed. "You still remember." Callas sang, her voice rose and fell, and Stein sped up and slowed down, I had to laugh, too, and briefly touched his cheek. His skin was unusually bristly. I wondered what was usual. Stein said, "See," and I saw that he immediately regretted it.

After Angermünde he turned off the road, stopping in front of a driveway that led to a low building from the sixties; he braked so hard that I hit my head against the windshield. Disappointed and alarmed, I asked, "Is this it?" and Stein was pleased at that. He slithered over the icy concrete with exaggerated movements, approaching a woman in a housedress who had just stepped out of the front door. A pale child clung to her. I rolled down the car window, and heard him call out with jovial warmth, "Mrs. Andersson!"— I had always hated the way he dealt with people of this type. He offered her his hand and she did not take it, but dropped a huge bunch of keys into it. "There's no water when it's freezing," she said. "Supply line's broken. But they're going to turn the power on next week." The child hanging on to her housedress began to bawl. "Doesn't matter," Stein said, slid back to the car, stopped at my rolled-down window, and rotated his pelvis elegantly and obscenely. He said, "Come on baby, let the good times roll." I said, "Stein, stop that," I felt myself blushing. The child let go of the woman's dress and took an amazed step toward us.

"They used to live in it," Stein said as he restarted the engine. He reversed back onto the road. The snow was falling more heavily now, I turned around and watched the woman and the child standing in the illuminated rectangle of the doorway until the house disappeared behind a curve. "They're mad because they had to get out a year ago. I didn't kick them out, it was the owner from Dortmund. I only bought it. As far as I'm concerned they could have stayed on."

I said, uncomprehending, "But they're disgusting," and Stein said, "What's disgusting?" and threw the bunch of keys into my lap. I counted the keys, there were twenty-three, small ones and very large ones, all old, with beautifully curved handles, and I sang under my breath, "The key to the stable, the key to the attic, the one for the gate, for the barn, for the parlor, for the milking room, mailbox, cellar, and garden gate," and suddenly—without really wanting to—I understood Stein's enthusiasm, his anticipation, his excitement. I said, "It's nice that we're driving there together, Stein."

He refused to look at me and said, "In any case, from the veranda you can see the sun going down behind the church tower. And we'll be there soon. After Angermünde comes Canitz, and Canitz is where the house is."

Canitz was worse than Lunow, worse than Templin, worse than Schönwalde. Gray, cowering houses on both sides of the curving country road, many windows boarded up, no store, no bakery, no inn. The snow flurries were getting heavier. "A lot of snow here, Stein," I said, and he said, "Of course," as though he had bought the snow along with the house. When the village church appeared on the left side of the street, beautiful and red with a round bell tower, Stein started to make an odd humming sound, like a fly bumping against closed windows in the summer. He turned onto a small cross street, brought the car to a stop, took his hands off the steering wheel with an emphatic gesture, and said, "That's it."

I looked out the car window and thought, "That's it for another five minutes." The house looked as though it were about to cave in suddenly and soundlessly. I climbed out and shut the car door carefully, feeling as though every vibration might be too much, and Stein also walked on tiptoe toward the house. The house was a ship. It sat at the edge of this Canitz village street like a proud vessel beached in times long gone by. It was a large, two-story country manor house of red brick; it had a skeletonized gable roof with two wooden horse's heads, one on each end. Most of the windows no longer had glass panes. The crooked veranda was held together only by dense ivy, and cracks as wide as a thumb ran through the brickwork. The house was beautiful. It was *the* house. And it was a ruin.

The gate from which Stein was trying to remove a "For Sale" sign collapsed with a plaintive sound. We climbed over it, then I stood still, startled by the expression on Stein's face, and saw him disappear behind the ivy on the veranda. Soon afterward a window frame fell off the house, and Stein's excited face appeared amid the jagged glass of one pane, lit up by a kerosene lamp.

145

"Stein!" I shouted. "Get out of there! It's going to collapse!"

"Come in!" he yelled back. "It's *my house!*"

I briefly asked myself why that should be reassuring, then stumbled over garbage bags and trash onto the veranda. Its boards groaned and the ivy immediately swallowed all light. I pushed the vines aside in disgust, and then Stein's ice-cold hand pulled me into the hall. I grabbed it. I grabbed for his hand; suddenly I didn't want to lose his touch again, and especially not the glow of his wretched little kerosene lamp. He was humming, and I followed him.

He pushed all the shutters open toward the garden, and we saw the last of the daylight through the red splinters of glass in the doors. The keys, heavy in my jacket pocket, were totally unnecessary: all the doors either stood open or weren't even there. Stein held up the lamp, pointed, described, stood breathlessly before me, as if trying to say something, but said nothing as he pulled me along. He stroked the banisters and door handles, tapped on walls, picked at the wallpaper, and marveled at the dusty plaster underneath. He said, "You see?" and, "Feel this," and "How do you like this?" I didn't have to answer him, he was talking to himself. He knelt on the kitchen floor, wiped the filth off the tiles, and muttered. I clung to him all this time, yet I no longer existed. Some kids had left their marks on the walls —*I wanna hold your hand. I was here. Mattis. No risk, no fun.* I said, "I wanna hold your hand."

Stein turned toward me, suddenly confused, and said, "What?"

I said, "Nothing."

He grabbed my arm and pushed me along in front of him, kicked the back door out into the garden, and dragged me down a few stairs.

"Here."

"What do you mean—here?"

"Everything!" said Stein. I had never seen him so unrestrained and brash. "A Brandenburg lake, chestnut trees in the yard, one and a half acres of land, you can plant your goddamned grass here, and mushrooms and hemp and shit. Plenty of room, you understand? Plenty of room. I'll build you a salon and a billiard room and a smoking room, and separate rooms for everyone, and a big table in back of the house for your shitty meals, and then you can get up and walk over to the Oder and snort coke until your skull splits."

He twisted my head roughly toward the land, but it was too dark, I could scarcely make out anything. I began to shiver.

I said, "Stein, please. Stop."

He stopped. He was silent, we looked at each other. We were breathing hard and almost in the same rhythm. Slowly he put his hand on my face, I flinched, and he said, "All right. All right, all right. OK."

I stood still. I didn't understand a thing. Remotely I understood something, but it was still much too far away. I was exhausted and weary, I thought of the others and felt a passing anger that they had left me here alone, that no one else was here to protect me from Stein, not Christiane, nor Anna, nor Heinze. Stein shuffled his feet and said, "I'm sorry."

I said, "Doesn't matter. Never mind."

He took my hand, his hand was warm now and soft, and said, "So then, the sun behind the church tower."

On the veranda he wiped snow off the stairs and invited me to sit down. I sat down. I felt incredibly cold. I took the lighted cigarette he held out to me and smoked, staring at the church tower behind which the sun had already set. I had a guilty feeling, as if I should be saying something forward-looking, something optimistic. I felt confused. I said, "I'd take the ivy off the veranda in the summer. Otherwise we can't see anything if we want to sit here and drink wine."

Stein said, "Will do."

I was sure he hadn't been listening. Sitting next to me, he seemed tired. He looked at the cold, empty, snowy street; I thought of summer, of that hour in Heinze's garden in Lunow, and wished that Stein would look at me once more the way he had back then, but I hated myself for thinking it.

I said, "Stein, would you please tell me something? Could you please explain something to me?"

Stein flicked his cigarette into the snow, looked at me, and said, "What should I tell you? This is one possibility, one of many. You can go with it, or you can drop it. I can go with it, or I can drop it and go somewhere else. We could do it together or pretend that we never knew each other. Doesn't matter. I only wanted to show it to you, that's all."

I said, "You paid 80,000 marks to show me a possibility? One of many? Did I understand that correctly, Stein? What's the point?"

He didn't react. He leaned forward and looked hard at the street. I followed his gaze. The street was dim, and the last light reflected by the snow made it hard to see. Someone was standing on the other side of the street. A figure was standing about fifteen feet away; I squinted and sat up, and it turned and walked into the shadows between two houses. A garden gate banged. I was convinced I had recognized the child from Angermünde—the pale, dumb child that had clung to the woman's housedress.

Stein got up and said, "Let's go."

I said, "Stein—the child. From Angermünde. Why is it standing around here on the street, watching us?" I knew he wouldn't answer. He held the car door open for me. I stood in front of him, waiting for something, for a touch, a gesture. I thought: But *you* always wanted to be with us.

Stein said coolly, "Thanks for coming with me."

Then I got into the car.

I no longer remember what kind of music we listened to on the way back. In the following weeks I saw Stein only rarely. The lakes froze over, we bought ice skates; at night we roamed through the woods and out over the ice carrying torches. We listened to Paolo Conte on Heinze's boom box, took ecstasy, and read aloud the best parts from Bret Easton Ellis's *American Psycho*. Falk kissed Anna, Anna kissed me, and I kissed Christiane. Sometimes Stein was there too. He kissed Henrietta, and whenever he did, I looked away. We avoided each other. He hadn't told anybody that he had finally bought the house, or that he had driven out there with me. I didn't either. I didn't think about the house, but sometimes, when we threw our ice skates and torches into the trunk of his cab before driving back to the city, I saw roofing paper, wallpaper, and paint inside.

In February, Toddi fell through the ice on Lake Griebnitz. Heinze was skating wildly across the ice, holding up his torch and shouting, "What fun this is! What a great time we're having, I can't believe it!" He was completely drunk, and Toddi slid along behind him, and we called out, "Say blue, Toddi! Say it!" and then there was a crack, and she disappeared.

We stood still. Heinze, his mouth open, skated a terrific loop. The ice hummed, and wax dripped hissing from our torches. Falk sped off on his skates, tripping, while Anna tore off her scarf, and Christiane stupidly covered her face with her hands and screamed weakly. Falk crept along on his belly, Heinze was out of sight. Falk yelled for Toddi, and Toddi yelled back. Anna threw out her scarf, Henrietta clung to Falk's feet, I stopped moving. Stein also stopped. I took the lighted cigarette he held out to me. He said, "Blue," I said, "Cold," and then we began to laugh. We laughed, doubled over, and lay down on the ice, and the tears ran down our cheeks; we laughed and couldn't stop, not even when they brought Toddi back, wet and shivering, and Henrietta said, "Are you crazy, or what?"

In March, Stein disappeared. He didn't turn up for Heinze's thirtieth birthday or for Christiane's premiere, or for Anna's concert either. He was gone, and when Henrietta naively asked where he was, everyone else shrugged their shoulders. I didn't shrug, but I didn't say anything either. A week later his first postcard arrived. It was a photo of the village church in Canitz, and on the back it said:

The roof is waterproofed. The child is blowing its nose, doesn't speak, is always here. The sun is dependable, I smoke when it's setting. I've planted something you can eat. I'll cut the ivy when you come. Remember, you still have the keys.

After that, postcards arrived regularly. I waited for them, and when they failed to come, I was disappointed. They always had photos of the church, and four or five sentences like little riddles, sometimes nice, sometimes incomprehensible. Stein often wrote "when you come." He didn't write "Come." I decided to wait for "Come," and then I would go. In May there was no card, but there was a letter. I looked at Stein's large, clumsy handwriting on the envelope, crawled back into bed with Falk, and tore open the envelope. Falk was still asleep and snoring. Inside there was a newspaper clipping from the *Angermünder Anzeiger*. Stein had scribbled the date on the back. I pushed Falk's sleep-warmed body aside, unfolded the article, and read:

REGIONAL NEWS

Friday night the former manor house in Canitz burned down to its foundation. The owner, a Berliner who bought the eighteenth-century house half a year ago and restored it, has been reported missing since. The cause of the fire has not yet been established. So far the police are not ruling out arson.

I read it three times. Falk stirred. I stared at the article, then at Stein's handwriting on the envelope, and back again. The postmark was from Stralsund. Falk woke up, looked at me apathetically for a moment, then reached for my wrist, and with the nasty cunning of fools, asked:

"What's that?"

I pulled my hand away, climbed out of bed, and said, "Nothing." I went to the kitchen and stood stupidly in front of the stove for ten minutes. The clock above the stove ticked. I ran into the back room, pulled out the desk drawer, and added the envelope to the other cards and the bunch of keys. I thought, "Later."

Translated from the German by Margot Bettauer Dembo

6

DIETER APPELT

VIA LEWANDOWSKY

JOHN BOCK

JOHANNES KAHRS

OLAV WESTPHALEN

Olav Westphalen, *Tree House*, Kunstverein Kassel, 1996.

Gone are the days when the art audience's threshold could be battered by Via Lewandowsky's piss pictures or by his filibustering perorations, which ended in puking (carrot juice served as the brightly colored stimulus). From the mid-eighties on, he gave free rein to his annoyance at art that was being big-brothered by East German politicos. Lewandowsky and his like-minded colleagues called themselves "auto-perforation artists"—a sarcastic reference to self-destructing veins of anarchism. They used their performances and shock-action strategies to rattle the false-front culture of the Communist state. Instead of socialist realism, the hollow propaganda art that had been declared the norm, Lewandowsky introduced "reproductive painting"—not to be confused with the clichéd images cribbed from the mass media and multi-fabricated by the exponents of pop art in the sixties. Lewandowsky took antiquated pictures and so thoroughly transformed them for his subversive philosophy that the motifs, recycled as fragments, were in tune with the utterly shattered experience of the world and the body in this modern, technological era.

Birgit Sonna

Translated from the German by Joachim Neugroschel

During the 1980s there emerged in East Berlin, and in many other cities of the German Democratic Republic, a remarkable number and variety of self-published and illegal artists' journals. An adventurous and lively cross between rare art books and cheap brochures, they contained original artworks along with all sorts of hand- or typewritten texts, in often barely decipherable carbon copies; there were no copy machines and hardly any computers. The writing ranged from poetry and fragments of novels to film scripts, absurd correspondence with state institutions and insightful essays on art and literature.

Feverishly manufactured behind crumbling facades and often in bugged apartments belonging to artists and writers, these journals were then sent on their precarious way, to circulate in a growing scene of eager readers that included the state's secret police, the Stasi. They were meant to be passed by hand, a sort of mail-art delivered in person, and were not meant to be sold, although occasional proceeds were known to come in handy for the purchase of more paper. Around the time the Wall came down,

museums, libraries and book lovers began to pay serious attention to these shabby and exotic treasures, and their prices rose tremendously. Historians, art collectors, and nostalgists hurried to purchase their own battered piece of history, a GDR souvenir with the resistance's authentic fingerprints.

The impulse behind these publications was the desire to create a network and public forum for the many artists and writers who were not allowed, or who themselves refused to publish or show their work in the censorship-ridden state venues. It was not by accident that these collaborative journals surfaced at around the same time that punk rock erupted in East German courtyards, underground clubs, and the supposedly protective spaces of the church. The bands' names and the titles of some of the magazines shared the same passion and defiance. Among the journals in East Berlin were *Schaden (Damage)*, some issues of which came with cassettes featuring the latest independent band, *Herzattacke (Heart Attack)*; *Entwerter/Oder (Devaluator/Or—*a word play with entweder/oder meaning either/or); *Koma-Kino (Coma Cinema)*; *Ariadnefabrik (Ariadne Factory)*; *Bizarre Städte (Bizarre Cities)*; and *Verwendung (Use)*. In other cities they had names like *UND (And)*; *U.S.W. (And So On)*; *Reizwolf* (an invented word meaning provocative wolf and an adaptation of *Reißwolf*, which means paper shredder); and *Anschlag (Attack*, but also public notice).

However, almost none of the mostly young publishers and contributors claimed a political agenda—on the contrary, aside from a few exceptions, they wanted to get as far away from politics as possible. But the fact that these journals existed outside the official culture industry was, in itself, a statement of opposition. Those involved with putting out the journals had set out to experiment freely with the contours of language, visual and aesthetic concepts, as well as with their artistic heritage. What they arrived at was full-flavored, snappy and in-your-face, and thus a radical raid on the encrusted, lifeless language of the authorities and on the socialist realist art they favored.

LEFT:
Entwerter/Oder (Either/Or) #13. Edition of 15, Berlin, 1985
Cover: 3-color linoprint by Klaus Storde

RIGHT:
Entwerter/Oder (Either/Or) #68. Edition of 30, Berlin, 1998.
Cover: Photograph by Claus Bach on cardboard

These publications were created in constant friction with the dogma of the state and its institutions, a condition that largely defined their form and content. The circumstances of their production were both comic and tragic, a schizophrenic mess that, as it turned out, provided enormous creative potential. Bound between individually painted, drawn, or silk-screened cardboard covers was refreshing evidence of a desire to collaborate and inspire. Ironically, a major encouragement for such intense dialogue between the different artistic fields—a climate in some respects reminiscent of German Expressionism—was unintentionally supplied by the government

itself. In 1979 a tightened printing law required state permission for every text unless it was part of a pictorial structure. It was not so easy to disregard such laws, which often resulted in prison sentences or overnight deportations to the West. To circumvent this decree, artists and writers simply joined together, painting over poems or writing across images. Some journals devoted themselves to the documentation of collective projects that involved, besides artists and writers, musicians, dancers, filmmakers and many others.

The cultivation of these highly contagious creative communities was perhaps their authors' greatest achievement. However, in the beginning of the 1990s, two of the main instigators, along with several others actively involved, were uncovered as longtime informers for the Stasi. Now, there is still a debate as to how to define this scene: Was it a counterculture, an autonomous culture, or a supplemental culture? Was it the underground or the alternative? It was probably a little of each—a robust alternative, but a much infiltrated one. It would be an error, however, to dismiss these ventures as Stasi-staged manipulation. They were under surveillance because they existed, not the other way around.

Has some of the collaborative spirit survived? There are, in fact, many examples in Berlin. The artist Via Lewandowsky and writer Durs Grünbein, who have worked together since the mid-1980s, are still collaborating on projects. A publishing house and printing company, the Druckhaus Galrev in Prenzlauer Berg, brings out a remarkable palette of idiosyncratic editions, magazines (such as *Warten*), and books in which not only former East Germans, but international artists and writers meet between beautifully crafted covers. The author Uwe Warnke, founder of *Entwerter/Oder*, the most enduring of all the journals mentioned (in production since 1982), pushes his passions further in *Warnke Verlag*, where he publishes sharp-tongued experimental writing, found and visual poetry, as well as graphic editions. And he still puts out *Entwerter/Oder*, now at issue No. 75. Faithful to the well-tried tradition, invitations to contribute are sent to artists and writers as follows: "At least two pages (more no problem), format A4, photographs and graphics should be originals, all contributions in editions of thirty and signed."

It has been said before, but it's worth repeating: How fortunate for all of us East Germans that times have changed and we can be challenged and judged by wider objectives.

FILM

DANIEL EISENBERG

DOGFILM

JOHN BURGAN

Persistence

Film in 24 absences/presences/prospects

PRESENCE (V):

USAF FILES 24844 & SFP 186

GERMANY 1945/6

ABOVE:

Daniel Eisenberg, stills from *Persistence*, 1997.
16mm, color, 84 min.

(forbidden knowledge)

While filming at the Stasi Headquarters, I observed this man sitting motionless at a table, listening to a tape and silently crying. The tape looped over and over, filling the room with the voice of Erich Mielke, the former chief officer at the Stasi. Mielke was in prison at the time, being held on charges of conspiracy against the police in the 1930s.

Who was this man at the table? A Stasi officer himself, only a few months earlier powerful and feared, and now an outcast? Or a victim of the Stasi, someone who had been sent away for years for an invented crime? Sometime later the man approached me and spoke into my ear. He reeked of vodka.

  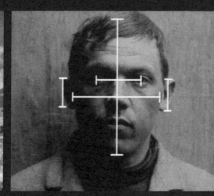

Following the American models of Act Up and Paper Tiger Television, dogfilm mixes veins of art, sociology, and political activism. Founded in 1991 as a media collective, dogfilm has been an active participant in the Berlin art and club scene, and many of its social themes spring from a pop culture context. The first projects were produced together with an interdisciplinary organization by the name of Botschaft e.V. (Message), dedicated to the documentation of urban identity in Berlin after reunification. The exhibition *Dromomania* examined how public space has changed with the new, faster forms of communication used by the service industry (such as electronic networks and telebanking). In

another project, a radio transmitter was installed at the Hamburg Kuntstverein, broadcasting on themes such as migration and urban planning.

Dogfilm now limits itself to the medium of video. Since 1993, its central concern has been the debate over political asylum. The film *Juristische Körper* (*Juristic Bodies*), 1995, shows in detail the care Germany takes in regulating the official national identity of its citizens. Improvements in forgery-proof passports through technology such as genetic fingerprinting have helped strengthen immigration control while simultaneously perfecting the system of tracking down "illegal" persons. The film takes the position that developments such as genetic

fingerprinting do not aim to protect German citizens, but rather serve primarily to identify undesirable foreigners. Juxtaposed with footage of surveillance technicians at Berlin's registry office, a woman from Latin America explains the difficulties in surviving without papers: It's almost impossible to find work; don't get sick, because you cannot go to a doctor . . . and so on. According to the film, the state makes policies based on identity, not on individuals, and illegality is an arbitrarily determined concept—one that depends on how the state interprets individual fates.

In the film *killer.Berlin.doc*, which had its premiere at the 1999 Berlin Film Festival, the terms are reversed: Ten people take part in a game in which each is assigned another's name—and the task of killing that person. From this constellation the biographies of the participants are pieced together like criminological studies. The fiction of hit man assignments is transposed with vérité profiles of the participants: Berliners in their thirties in a capital city at its departure, where the push for existence has replaced reunification utopia.

Harald Fricke

Translated from the German by John Hamilton

LEFT:
Dogfilm, stills from *Juristic Bodies*, 1995. Color, 48 min.
ABOVE:
Dogfilm, stills from *killer.Berlin.doc*, 1998. Color, 74 min.

November of 1989, I was in London watching the fall of the Berlin Wall on television. The city coming together seemed to open up a fault in me. Then, a memory: Berlin, summer 1967, home-movie images I had often seen as a child. Something was missing. I had no words to describe this feeling; I just knew I had to go back to the beginning.

A man carries an image of his childhood around with him for years like an unopened parcel; he doesn't have a way to express feelings that lack a name. German gives us a list of words which have that is almost a hunger, is the word that started this crazy journey: *Sehnsucht*.

There is something weird about the clocks in Berlin. After reunification they discovered that the electric current in the East fluctuated so much that public clocks were always off by different amounts; nowhere could you tell what hour it was. And this still seems to be the problem in Berlin: the city may have been reunified in space, but not in time. Every post-'89 commentator tells of the "wall in peoples'

passed into English: *Weltschmerz*—the pain of the world; *Schadenfreude*—joy at another's misfortune; *Doppelgänger*—ghostly double. The unwieldy compounds, monsters such as *Vergangen-heitsbewältigung*—perhaps best defined as coming to terms with the past—are still strangely foreign to most speakers of English. But there are some words that resist translation, shorter words that, though they can be understood, express feelings that are themselves untranslatable. What the Germans call *Heimat* is not a place to be found on any map, but home and homeland, the place where you stop running. And the single most beautiful word in the entire language, meaning desire, longing, a yearning heads" or "the wall in peoples' hearts." But the image of the city should be of two clocks, running at different speeds, never catching up with each other.

The city is split, there are two of everything: two observatories, two state libraries, even two zoos. But if I ever get lost in Berlin, there it is, the TV tower at the center. Casting its shadow over the Scheunenviertel— the Finstere Medine, the dark district—it conceals a wound at the heart of Berlin. It's a big, bloodshot, unblinking eye looking out over the city. I see it and it sees me, watching me wherever I am.

John Burgan

ABOVE:

John Burgan, stills from *Memory of Berlin*, 1998. 16mm, Color & black-and-white, 76 min.

THE LONG CORRIDORS OF THE WOMEN'S DORMITORY

EMINE SEVGI ÖZDAMAR

ON THE TRAIN FROM ISTANBUL I spent several nights running back and forth along the corridor, looking at all the women on their way to Germany to become workers. They had rolled their stockings down below the knees, and the thick elastic bands left dark marks on their skin. I got a clearer picture of the distance still to go from their bare knees than from the signs on the railway stations we passed, which had names I couldn't read. One woman said, "What an endless journey!" Some of the women smoked, looking into one another's faces. Those of us who didn't smoke looked out the window.

One woman said, "It's gotten dark again."

Another said, "It's no darker than yesterday."

Each cigarette seemed to push the train forward more quickly. We hadn't undressed for three days and three nights. The floor was bare except for a few shoes, which were shaking along with the train. Whenever one of the women wanted to go to the bathroom she would quickly pick up any pair of shoes and hop clumsily to the clogged toilets. I was looking for women who resembled my mother. When I saw that one of them had shoes with heels like hers, I put on my sunglasses and began to cry softly. How lovely my mother's shoes had looked beside mine in Istanbul. How easily the two of us used to slip our shoes on and go to Liz Taylor movies, or to the opera.

Mama, Mama.

I thought to myself, I'll get there, get a bed, and never stop thinking about her. That will be my job. I began to cry harder, and then I got angry, as though it were my mother who had left me. I hid my face behind a book of Shakespeare's plays.

The train arrived in Munich shortly before dawn. The women whose shoes had been off for days had puffy feet, and so they sent the others out to buy cigarettes and chocolate. *Çikolata-Çikolata.*

I lived with many other women in a women's hostel, but we called it the "ostel." When I arrived in Berlin, the city seemed like an endless building. I came out the door of the train with the other women and went into the mission office at the railway station. Rolls-coffee-milk-nuns-neon lights; then out the mission door and into the bus; then out of the bus and into the Turkish women's ostel; then out of the ostel and into Hertie's department store at Hallesches Tor. To get from the women's ostel to Hertie's, we had to walk beneath an overpass for the S-Bahn. There were groceries on the bottom floor of Hertie's. One day, three of us girls from the ostel wanted to buy sugar, salt, eggs, toilet paper, and toothpaste, but we didn't know the words. To describe sugar, we mimed drinking coffee in front of the sales clerk, then said, "schak, schak." To describe salt, we spat on Hertie's floor, stuck our tongues out, and said, "eeee." To describe eggs, we turned our backs toward the sales clerk, waddled our behinds, and said: "Gak gak gak." She gave us sugar, salt, and eggs, but not the toothpaste. Instead we got cleansers for bathroom tiles. And so my first German words were "schak schak, eeee, gak, gak, gak."

We all worked in a radio factory, where we had to wear magnifying glasses over our right eyes. In the evening, when we got back to the ostel, we looked at each other or at the potatoes we were peeling with our right eyes; our left eyes were always scrunched up and half-closed. We even slept with them scrunched up. When we got up at five o'clock in the morning and searched in the half-light for our pants or skirts, I could see that the other women, like me, were using only their right eyes. We began to trust our right eyes more than our left eyes. With our right eyes behind the magnifying glasses, and pincers in our hands, we would bend the thin wires in the little radios. The wires were like spider legs—very fine, almost invisible without the glasses. The factory boss's name was Herr Schering. The women called him "Sherin" or "Sher." Then they added "Herr" to "Sher," and to many of the women he became "Herschering" or "Herscher." We never saw him, but I tried to imagine him in the face of the interpreter, who brought his words to us as Turkish words: "Herscher said you . . "

On November 10th, the anniversary of Atatürk's death, Herscher wanted us to stand up for a few minutes at exactly five past nine, just as we had in Turkey. So at five past nine, we stood in front of our machines, our right eyes bigger than our left eyes. The women who wanted to cry did so with their right eyes, their tears running across their right breasts and down onto their right shoes. We made the floor of a radio factory in Berlin wet with tears for Atatürk's death. But the neon lights quickly dried the tears. Some women had forgotten to remove the magnifying glass from their right eye, and tears gathered inside.

At work our lives were a kind of still-life image: our fingers, the neon light, the tweezers, and the little radios with their spidery wires. We had separated ourselves from the sounds of the world, and from our own bodies; our spines, breasts, and hair seemed to disappear. Sometimes our noses ran, and we kept putting off the moment when we had to sniffle, as though the sound would destroy the larger picture in which we lived. When the Turkish interpreter's shadow fell across the picture, the image tore open and the world returned. When I looked at her face I could hear the sounds of the airplanes somewhere in the sky, or the ringing echo of a metal object that had fallen on the factory floor.

Like a mailman waiting for a registered letter to be signed, the interpreter, having finished translating Herscher's messages, would wait for the women to say OK. When one of the women used the Turkish word "tamam" instead of the English "OK," the interpreter repeated OK until the woman said it, too. If a woman made the interpreter wait while working with her tweezers, or inspecting a radio with her magnifying glass, the interpreter would stand there, blowing the hair from her forehead with noticeable impatience, until she finally heard an OK.

OK made its way into the women's ostel as well: "You'll clean the room tomorrow, OK?"

"Tamam."

"Say OK."

"OK."

170

Ever since I was a child in Istanbul, I had prayed for the souls of the dead before I went to sleep. My mother and grandmother often spoke about those who had recently died, and my mother would say: "If you forget the souls of the dead, their souls will feel pain." First I said my daily prayers, then the names of all the dead I had heard about, usually people I hadn't known. During my first nights in Berlin I remembered to pray for the dead, but since we had to get up early, I fell asleep before I had finished calling out their names, and in that way I lost my dead in Berlin. I thought to myself, when I go back to Istanbul, I will start calling out their names again.

I had forgotten the dead, but I hadn't forgotten my mother. I lay down in bed to think her. But I had no idea how to; it was much easier to think about falling in love with a movie actor, about how I would kiss him.

But how does anyone think about a mother?

Some nights, as in a film shown backward, I imagined myself running from the door of the ostel to the train that had taken me here. The train ran backward too. The trees ran backward past the train, but the journey was too long, I only got as far as Austria, where the mountains had their heads in the mist, and it was hard to imagine a train running backward. Here I would fall asleep. I noticed, though, that when I was hungry, or when I scratched my finger until it hurt, I thought about my mother. I thought to myself, this pain is my mother. And so I often went to bed hungry or with aches in my fingers.

Rezzan, who slept above me, didn't eat right either. She too was thinking about her mother. She would stay awake a long time, turning from left to right in the dark, moving her pillow from one end of the bed to the other. After a while she would begin again, turning from left to right, from right to left. Below her I thought of my mother with half my head, and with the other half I began to think of Rezzan's mother.

Two cousins from Istanbul slept in the two other bunk beds. They were working in the factory so that they could go to the university eventually. One of them had two plaits, deep pockmarks on her face, and smelly breath. The other cousin was beautiful, and often sent the one with the smelly breath to the post office and to Hertie's. One morning we saw the beautiful cousin push the smelly one down on the table. She rolled her sleeves up, removed her belt, and began to whip her cousin.

Rezzan and I said, "What are you doing?"

She cried, "The whore went to the post office and was late coming back."

We said, "But she doesn't have wings! Did you expect her to fly? She didn't come back slowly."

"You two mind your own business. Mind your own business. Mind your own business." Each time she said those words, she hit her smelly cousin on the back, looking straight into our eyes. Her pupils twisted like a light gone mad, her right eye bigger than her left.

That night, when we were all in bed, the smelly girl climbed into the top bunk with her beautiful cousin. They pulled the eiderdown out of the duvet, let it fall to the ground, crept into the cover as though it were a sleeping bag, and buttoned it up. In this way, buttoned up in a bag, they kissed each other— *smooch smooch*—and made love. The rest of us listened without stirring.

Across from the ostel was the Hebbel Theater, lit up at night with a blinking advertisement that cast light into our room. Intermittently, when the sign went out, I could hear the *smooch smooch* of the kisses in the darkness. When the sign was on, I could see curlers gleaming on the pillows, and shoes on the linoleum floor.

Rezzan never took her shoes off at night, but lay in bed fully dressed. She held her toothbrush in her hand as she slept, and the toothpaste lay under her pillow. Like me, Rezzan wanted to be an actress. Some nights in the blinking light from the Hebbel Theater, we spoke softly about acting. Rezzan asked, "Which role would you like to play? Ophelia?"

"No, I'm too thin for Ophelia. But perhaps Hamlet."

"Why Hamlet?"

"I don't really know why. And you?"

"The woman in *Cat on a Hot Tin Roof* by Tennessee Williams."

"I don't know anything about Tennessee Williams."

"He was a homosexual, and he left school for the sake of the theater, like us. Did you know that Harold Pinter left school, too? Do you know *The Servant* by Harold Pinter?"

"No."

Rezzan fell silent. Under the blinking lights from the Hebbel Theater, the curlers gleamed in their beds.

In the morning there were no lights on at the Hebbel Theater, but there was a bread store near the ostel that always had its lights on, and as we waited for the bus our shadows fell gently on the snow. Some of the women arrived at the bus stop carrying full cups of coffee, and when the bus came and the door opened—*tiss pam*—they poured out what was left. After the bus picked us up, the only traces left of us in the snow were footprints and coffee stains. One morning the headline in the newspaper box in front of the bread store read: HE WAS NO ANGEL. From the window on the right side of the bus I could see the demolished Anhalter railway station. It stood next to the Hebbel Theater, opposite our ostel. The Turkish word for demolished can also mean insulted, so we called it "the insulted railway station."

Shortly before we got to the factory, the bus had to drive up a long steep street, and we all toppled backward. Then came a bridge, where we toppled forward, and every damp morning I saw two women there in the half-light, walking hand in hand. Their hair was cropped short, and they wore skirts and shoes with run-down heels. Their knees must have been freezing. Behind them I could see the canal and the dark factory buildings. The asphalt on the bridge was broken, and rain collected in its holes. They never looked at the bus, nor did they look at one another. It seemed as though they were the only people alive in this city. I didn't know whether they belonged to the night or the morning. Were they coming from the factory or were they going to the cemetery?

At the radio factory the bus doors opened, and the wind blew snow into the bus. It melted on the hair, eyelashes, and coats of the women. The factory yard swallowed us. The snow was falling more heavily, and the women huddled together before walking into the luminescent flakes. It seemed like someone was shaking stars on them. Their coats and skirts made soft fluttering sounds beneath the sound of the factory horns. With one wet hand they pressed down their time cards—*tink tink tink*—and with the other they shook the snow from their coats, wetting the cards and the floor in front of the porter's office. The porter rose slightly from his chair to greet us. I tried out the German sentence I had learned from that day's headline: "Hewasnoangel."

"Morning, morning," he said.

For the first few weeks we lived in transit between the ostel door, Hertie's door, the bus door, the radio factory door, the factory toilet door, the ostel table, and the green iron factory table. Soon after the women had found the things they were looking for at Hertie's and the right name for their bus stop—at first they had thought the name of the bus stop was "Bus Stop"— they turned on the television in the ostel lounge for the first time.

The television had always been there. "We'll have a peek and see what's on," a woman said one night. From then on, many of the women watched figure skating in the lounge. When they returned from the factory, they put on their nightgowns and cooked macaroni, roast potatoes, and eggs in the kitchen. The sound of boiling water and sizzling food mixed with their reedy voices in the kitchen air, the room a rush of words, faces, and various dialects, the knives in their hands as they waited for the shared pots and pans, the water running nervously in the kitchen, and on a plate someone's spit.

The scene resembled a traditional Turkish shadow play, in which several figures converge on stage, each one speaking in her own dialect—a Turkish Greek, a Turkish Armenian, a Turkish Jew, a variety of Turks from various places and classes. Each misunderstands the other, but they carry on talking and acting, like the women in the ostel kitchen, who, though they could not understand one another, passed knives or pots along, or rolled up someone else's sleeve so it wouldn't get into the food. After the meal the director of the hostel, who was the only one who could speak German, came to inspect whether the kitchen was clean. Later the women took off their nightgowns and put their day clothes back on—some even applied makeup, as though they were going to the movies—and went into the ostel lounge, where they turned off the lights and sat down to watch the figure skaters. While the older women were sitting there in their movie theater, three of us—we were the youngest—left the ostel and went across the street to the food stand, which sold rissoles. The man there made them from horse meat, but we did not know this because we didn't speak any German. Rissole was our mothers' favorite food. Horse meat in hand then, we sat in front of the insulted railway station gazing at the weakly lit windows of the ostel. The insulted railway station was nothing more than a smashed wall and a porch with three gates. Whenever one of us made a sound in the night with the rissole bags, the others caught their breaths, not knowing whether it had been us or somebody else. We lost all sense of time at the insulted railway station. Once it had been full of people every morning, but the people who had used it were gone, and as we ran about I felt as though my life were already over. One night we went through a hole in the wall, and walked to the end of the property without speaking. Then we ran back together to the hole, which had perhaps once been the door of the insulted station, puffing as we ran. It was cold, and the night took our breath and turned it into thick smoke. When we went back to the street I looked behind me and saw the last wisps hanging in the air. The station looked as though it belonged to a different era. As the three of us went past the telephone booth standing in front of it, we spoke loudly, as though our parents could hear us in Türkiye.

Translated from the German by Mark Harman

GÜNTER KUNERT

Postwar Berlin

In backyards iron wheels
revolved floor
by floor
until they all burnt out
in the fire standstill
and stillness caved in
together with the empty shells
dead proletarians whirled up
with the unfettered wind
and drifted down once more
as a gray layer
over the city's remains.

Prinz Albert Strasse

In the middle of town
gaping earth
remnants of the tiled cellars
of torture workshops
for the creation
of history.

Translated from the German by Peter Constantine

7

HANS HAACKE

RENATA STIH &
FRIEDER SCHNOCK

RAFFAEL RHEINSBERG

EDWARD & NANCY
REDDIN KIENHOLZ

PAGE178-179:

Hans Haacke, *Berlin*, 1990. Berlin Wall seen from the East within the former "death strip."

RIGHT AND PAGE 181:

Hans Haacke, *Die Freiheit wird jetzt einfach gesponsert— aus der Portokasse (Freedom is now simply going to be sponsored — out of petty cash)*, Berlin, 1990.

HANS HAACKE

Freedom is now simply going to be sponsored—out of petty cash

In 1961, along the border to West Berlin, East Germany had carved out on its territory a barren stretch of land, delineated by two unscalable walls, electrified fences, dog runs and minefields. This "border of peace" was under constant surveillance by patrols and from watchtowers equipped with powerful searchlights. About 175 people trying to escape to the West died in what became known as "the death strip."

One of these watchtowers, near the Heinrich-Heine checkpoint, was chosen for this project. Its windows were newly fitted with tinted glass, reminiscent of the Palasthotel in East Berlin, a luxurious GDR guesthouse. Like the windows of West German police vans, the Palasthotel windows were protected against rock throwers by wire grills. The searchlight on the roof of the watchtower was replaced by a slowly rotating Mercedes-Benz "star," enclosed in a wire cage. Particularly at night, the neon symbol dominated the desolate area of the former death strip.

On the roof of the Europa Center, the tallest building in the heart of the fashionable shopping district of West Berlin, a matching, though much larger, Mercedes-Benz emblem has been rotating for years. Daimler-Benz is among those German corporations that vigorously promoted Hitler's rise to power. Its chairman and president were both members of the SS. Like other companies during the war, Daimler-Benz relied mostly on forced labor. The company prospered again after the war, and has since agreed to pay a compensation of 434 Deutsche marks to each of the forty-eight thousand laborers who worked during that period. Daimler-Benz, now part of DaimlerChrysler following its merger with Chrysler, is now one of Germany's wealthiest enterprises, its largest producer of defense material, and the country's most conspicuous sponsor of art exhibitions.

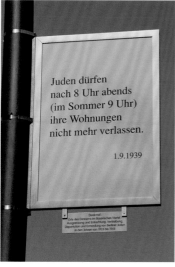

RENATA STIH AND FRIEDER SCHNOCK

Places of Remembrance, located in the Bayerische Viertel, a neighborhood in Berlin-Schöneberg, is a memorial to the large population of Jews who lived there under the Nazi regime. In June 1993, eighty brightly printed signs were mounted on lampposts throughout the neighborhood. The short black and white texts on the backs of these framed signs are condensed versions of rules and regulations passed from 1933 to 1945. These decrees, set by the National Socialists, systematically forced Jews out of daily life and gradually robbed them of their human rights.

THIS PAGE:

Raffael Rheinsberg. (left) *Säule (Column)*, Nationalgalerie Berlin
(West), 1982. **(right)** *Einreise (Immigration)* (detail), Berlin, 1991.

PAGE 182:

Renata Stih & Frieder Schnock, *Orte des Erinnerns (Places of
Remembrance)*, Berlin-Schöneberg, 1993. **Translation of sign
with clock:** Jews are not permitted to leave their apartments
after 8 p.m. (9 p.m. during the summer). September 1, 1939.
Translation of sign with shirts: Jews may not own or run retail
shops or mail order businesses. November 12, 1938.

EDWARD & NANCY REDDIN KIENHOLZ

In 1973 Edward Kienholz received a DAAD grant to work in Berlin and moved there with his wife, Nancy Reddin Kienholz, and their three children. For the next twenty-two years, they lived half the year in Idaho and half the year in Berlin. Kienholz liked Germany and had great empathy for Germans. He was fascinated by the tension between East and West, and made it the subject of the *Dumb Dumm Duel*. He thought it was terrific when the Wall came down, but he said, "Now I won't be able to get to my favorite hardware store." And it was true—as an American, he had an easier time getting into East Germany before reunification. After reunification, the traffic was terrible.

All three of Kienholz's works for Berlin were a real poke in the eye. He proposed the *Dumb Dumm Duel* for the 400th anniversary of Berlin. And *Still Live* (1974), the only one of the three that was ever realized, was a work in which you took your chances at being shot in the head. Firearms were absolutely illegal in Germany, and I don't know how he got them in. But Ed was never without guns. *The Berlin Fountain* was a crazy piece of public art. He wanted to build a see-through car wash in the middle of Berlin's Ernst-Reuter-Platz. Rooftop fountains would spray water onto a Mercedes-Benz car that moved back and forth upon a conveyer track as it was cleaned by constantly rotating brushes. The plans for this project, developed by him and Nancy, won the international Art in Construction (Kunst-am-Bau) Competition at Berlin's Technical University in 1983. It's astounding that they won that prize. *The Berlin Fountain* dealt with the theme of German guilt—like you see in movies, the killer forever trying to get the blood off his hands. Kienholz said, "I want a perfect Mercedes-Benz to be washed to pieces, and when it wears out, we'll get a new one." He thought Daimler-Benz should agree to keep on replacing the car. He loved the Mercedes-Benz. He thought it was the best car Germany made. The fountain seemed so innocent. But he wanted that beautiful car washed until the paint came off and it rusted away.

Walter Hopps

The Berlin Fountain was never realized. According to Nancy Kienholz, "We won a competition to build a fountain on Ernst-Reuter-Platz in Berlin. That was a long saga . . . let's just say The Berlin Fountain was never built and the six hundred thousand Deutsche marks allocated to the project disappeard into some bureaucratic pocket."

1961

GÜNTER GRASS

EVEN IF NO ONE PARTICULARLY CARES ANYMORE, I always say to myself looking back: Those were the best days of your life. You were given a job to do. You risked your life daily for more than a year. You were so scared you practically bit your fingernails off, but you met the danger head on, tried not to think about whether you were in for another disastrous semester. I was a student at the Technical University—even then I was interested in district heating—when from one day to the next the Wall went up.

People made an enormous fuss, rushed to rallies, staged protest marches in front of the Reichstag and elsewhere. Not me. First thing, in early August, I got Elke out. She was at a teacher-training college over there. All you needed was a West German passport, which was no problem in this case because we had her personal data and a picture. But by the end of the month we had to start working in groups and fiddling with the entry permits. I was the contact person. My passport, which was issued in Hildesheim—where I actually come from—worked for the next few weeks, but starting in September you had to hand in your entry permit as you left the eastern sector. We might have been able to make our own if somebody had smuggled out the kind of paper they used.

Not that people are interested nowadays. My kids certainly aren't. They either turn a deaf ear or say, "We know, Dad. You were real noble, your generation." Well, maybe my grandchildren will listen when I tell them how I got their grandma out and how she took an active part in "Operation Travel Bureau," our cover name. We were experts at getting the official stamps right. Some used hard-boiled eggs, others swore by finely sharpened matches. We were mostly students and mostly leftist, but we had our dueling society types, and a few—like me—who couldn't get excited about politics. It was election time in the West, and our Berlin mayor was a candidate for the Social Democrats, but I didn't vote for Brandt and the comrades, or for old man Adenauer either, because fancy words and ideologies didn't mean a thing to me; what counted was what you did. And our job was to "transfer," as we called it, passport pictures into West German and foreign passports— Swedish, Dutch, and others. Or to find contacts who would bring us passports with pictures and personal data—hair color, eye color, height, age —of the kind we needed. We also needed the right kind of newspapers, small change, used bus tickets—the odds and ends that, say, a Danish girl would be likely to have in her bag. It was tough work. And all of it free or at no cost.

Nowadays, when nothing is free, nobody can believe we didn't make a penny from it. Oh, a few held out their hands when we started digging the tunnel. It had a crazy history, the Bernauer Strasse project. What happened was that without our knowing it, an American TV company put up thirty thousand marks for the right to make a documentary about the tunnel. We'd dug for four long months through the Brandenburg sand—it was a hundred meters long, the tunnel—and when they filmed us smuggling thirty or so people, including grandmas and grandkids, into the West, it never occurred to me they'd put it on the air there and then. But that's what they did, and the tunnel would have been discovered in no time if it hadn't flooded—despite our expensive pumping equipment—shortly before the film was shown. No matter. We carried on elsewhere.

No, we had no casualties. I know, the papers were full of reports of people jumping from the third story of a building on the border, and landing on the pavement a hair's breadth from the safety net. A year after the Wall went up, a man by the name of Peter Fechter was shot barging his way through Checkpoint Charlie; he bled to death because nobody would come to his aid. We didn't need to worry, though, since we stuck to sure things. Still, I could tell you stories people didn't want to believe, even back then. About all the folks we took through the sewers, for instance. It stank to high heaven down there. We called one of these routes from the center of East Berlin to Kreuzberg "Glockengasse 4711," after the cologne, because all of us, the refugees and our people, had to wade knee-deep through raw sewage. I served later as cover, but not in the sense you might think. It was my job to wait until everybody had disappeared down the manhole, and then pull the cover back in place: the refugees themselves were so panic-stricken they'd forget to do it themselves. We had a similar problem at the Esplanadenstrasse runoff canal in the north of the city, when a few refugees let out a mighty cheer the moment they crossed over to the West. The East German police standing guard caught on and threw tear gas canisters down the hatch. Then there was the cemetery that had one edge in common with the Wall, so we dug a subterranean passageway up to the graves for our clientele, harmless-looking mourners with flowers and various paraphernalia, to vanish into. It worked just fine until a young woman who was taking her baby with her left a stroller at the camouflaged entrance to the passageway, which gave things away immediately.

Slips like that had to be factored in. But now let me tell you about a time when everything worked. Had enough, you say? I understand. I'm used to it. Things were different even a few years back, when the Wall was still up. I'd be having a Sunday beer with my coworkers from the district heating plant, and one or another of them would ask me, "What was it like, Ulli, when the Wall went up and you had to smuggle Elke into the West?" But nowadays nobody's interested, not here in Stuttgart at least. Because the Swabians never really grasped what it meant back in '61. So when the Wall came down all of a sudden . . . Actually, they liked having it there better. Because now that it's gone, they've got the solidarity tax to pay. So I'll shut up about it, even though it was the best time of my life, wading knee-deep through the sewage, crawling through the subterranean passageway. . . . My wife is right when she says, "You were another man back then. We had a real life. . . ."

Translated from the German by Michael Henry Heim

BRIGITTE OLESCHINSKI

BORN WITHOUT A HYMEN, EARS

hanging on your lips, I was your pleading
echo. I can only answer. When the wind catches me, I answer.
When the water in the empty foundations glistens, I answer.
You called me

like the squall of wind over the nettled slopes when a host
of crows ascends from the tops of the cranes. Your call
tore the voice from my body, I sang.

Shameful limbs, scattered
in singing. Only dogs

covered their tracks

THE SEVENTH PLAGUE

ate a path through the city, leveled streets, pavement, gardens
to a gray-green crunch, raked it

with sharply jointed legs. Between mugwort and noon, the sand boils
on the square, a residue of scales, razed, quiet as a rabbit.
There I found

the slow-worm's gutted skin. In the rubble chirps
a single fricative, it chirps and chirps

its name

SNOW, MORE AND MORE SNOW

sinks onto the tongues that say *peace plan*, gray
freezing over, dancing cones of titmouse and fir

behind rear window wires, more and more December
melts on caps and scarves in the Christmas storm, caramelized
lashes in a line in front of containers

for donations, more and more Christmas
falls down

onto the graveyard under more and more snow

HOW THE HOPPING BREATH

of the accordion drives the scraps down the pavement here—they all live
in the same neighborhood, the same defeat. Disguised. Between hubcap

and curb, an uptight helium fish, limp silver
from gill to gill, grins at the pale, filmy glue bag that wafts around
until it
finds the steps. Hesitates, turns upside down, and, on ballerina stumps,

dances upward because in the same torrent of air the fish
stands up and applauds

TO BE THE WASP AGAIN, WHICH IN THE MORNING

reels through an unfamiliar room, a soaring shimmer
above the construction site honeycombs, the truck routes fanning far

across the concrete, the pieces of laundry strewn
over the floor, it was bungee

on a silken thread, bun–

gee–

THE CLOTHES SWEAT

in the tunnel night, they flicker on the walls, flicker, flicker
on the walls, pyrotekel, mene-

script: like dragonflies

we flitted from Paris to Athens, from Athens to Berlin, a ribbed
fabric

doubled in love's flight, dragonflies, dragonflies
in a salvo

of love

Translated from the German by Andrew Shields

ALBERT OSTERMAIER

Tartar Titus is a dramatic parable about an engaged writer who desires to lend a political or a higher institutional power to his aesthetics and thereby to his artistic productivity. by his own specific means the writer wants to bring the ideology of this power, an ideology that has always been emphatically idealistic, closer to reality. and it is precisely in this realization, in this turning toward reality, that he fails. to be sure, on the surface, he gives this power all the necessary traits, namely the aesthetic charm of the classical masks, behind which he is able to hide the looming banality of unrestrained brutality in the most effectual of ways. however, he is a producer of a virtual reality with writing that stabilizes power and produces a compensating illusion; and so, by this very demonstration of power, which his ideas and aggressive ideals have inscribed with a beautiful appearance, the writer himself turns into a figure at risk. the completed work of art seeks to annihilate its creator and his manuscript.

this direct, personalized power, which should not be reduced to a single system, is not visible in the play; rather we simply see its henchman, for this, too, is exactly what titus was.

Tartar Titus shows how the shakespearean commander, titus andronicus, mutates into the militant poet, who "wrote roman letters over the gothic script." the meat-grinding beast now rips through paper, acquiring the ingredients for a tartar made of blood and word, a dish that should be offered as a divine feast for the commander. but titus himself is devoured by his own words. they devour his work and the hand that writes it. ultimately they even devour his "muse," lavinia, who soon will have no more hands with which to write, nor a tongue with which to speak.

how does it look when a poet prostitutes his muse of power, debasing her into raw material for rent? an orgy of power follows a revenge for power, and in turn is mercilessly followed by a requiem of impotence. a triptych. the poet of humanity turns into a cannibal. the poet of humanity, having been from time to time a cannibal in his civil capacity, now, through revenge on himself, finds his way back to a humanity that stays behind, mutilated, along with him.

Tartar Titus takes place in a timeless space that may encroach upon the present. the focus of the drama is not the unfolding of some plot. it is not a didactic play concerning politically engaged writing. the focus, rather, is language—language as the author's paradox, which causes him to experience power and impotence in equal doses.

I

TITUS: look at my hands see
           them what do they say
           are they a man's
           still or
           merely like the face
           of a man already dead
           touch them do you still sense
           the warmth that the hand
           shake of a friend gives
           you when he lets his
           rest in yours into
           his eye you look like only
           a friend can &
           tenderly almost from you
           he parts the look in his eye
           still a friend's the
           handshake eye to eye
           extending it feels like
           the hand that i show
           you are you laying it on
           your heart then mine beats
           too with yours
           or are you shuddering from
           the cold does your heart
           stay still because a dead hand
           approaches

even a murderer may have beautiful
hands what does it have to do with you
am i a murderer &
was it lovely to bathe
these hands in blood
or am i only an actor
who makes you afraid
laying his hand on all of you on
you & then you & on me
in the end i would hurry the
action along until
everyone gave the other his
hand & the life within it
you could read the life in mine
i'll read it out for you
this is my lifeline
do you see it the deep furrow
the wild river the ravine
that stretches here across
my hand & here in the other one
do you see the ax
what does that say what do you read
do you read your fate's power only
in the one or do you see it
in both & which one will be the
stronger & which
argument now fights its way through

does it have more weight here or sharpness
to convince is it the one that's
inscribed is it from a god
here into the tender
flesh he made a slip of the pen &
gives the ax
to the other then to correct
his mistakes by hand what
he himself wrote surely it's a
god when such errors are made
or is it only me who blunders
not knowing how to read the life
here & there how to destroy the ax
do you know the answer is the blow
worth it to you & life to me or is it
more likely reversed you take it from
me & i give you my hand for it
i don't know how i can
act when my hands are so
bound no exit comes to me
out of your number or out of my
thinking what should i do
tell me or i'll tell you
& do it too but we want
to talk about the other for
the hero gains what the dog
loses & i myself have both
& more than i could handle
won and lost once

i was a hero but now i
am the dog that i once was
a street urchin only & i am to you
a hero who went to the dogs
& through the dog
once again a hero for
only a man with teeth
to tear a man like a
wolf can build a city &
one establishes his fame
just as he builds his city &
directs man for man &
builds upon bones the memorial
of his power line for line
verse for verse & blood seals the
whole then to that work that
brings honor to one who is unreachable
in his power & look
again at my hands here
do they belong to a slave who dragged
stones are they rough cold & without
gleam a battlefield of wildly
lacerated skin that only hangs in strips
from these fingers or
do you see hands tender & fine with
skin made from parchment upon which
the words run & some
calluses also to withstand
foreign luck what do you

see here
will you not admit
on the one hand you see the slave
& on the other the master
on his hands the slave
never turns into a master but
through his hands the master turns into
a slave faster & faster than
he can understand but
tell me only what you see here
i'll keep on listening to your saying
& i won't trust my eyes
they're the eyes of a seer who
is not blind and therefore blind
for i once told myself
eye forget the hand and
happen what will it did
the eye held back seeing

II

the stage is diffused with red light, where the halls of a temple-bordello can be seen. in front the nine muses of antiquity pose as icons for sale—clio (history), calliope (epic, elegy), melpomene (tragedy), thalia (comedy), urania (astronomy), erato (love song, dance), euterpe (music, lyric), terpsichore (choral lyric, dance), polyhymnia (dance, pantomime, serious song). they are all dressed and made up as greek sculpture. among them and with the same motionlessness is lavinia, who at first is indistinguishable from the rest. behind her and off to the side stands titus's memorial statue, deceptively alive, masked as a pimp. titus himself takes the roles of the alternating johns.

LAVINIA: you're turning your child into a whore titus you're
                turning your child into a whoreson into the
                whoreson of titus the child
                who crept alone on the streets
                like a caterpillar along the walls so that no one
                might see it the ugly little abandoned
                one & with its wicked
                arts it wants to enchant becoming that which it
                already was & surely didn't want to see a
                butterfly with rubbed down wings
                who wears the colors of its clothing
                like a wound attracting everyone in the street
                a whoreson is what you're making out of me
                your child into a whore titus

TITUS: *silent*

1ST JOHN: lavinia how about a muse's kiss
                from your lips don't be ashamed
                my child what are you protecting i
                pay good money for every extra strophe let's
                try some cross rhymes come on
                my poem why make a fuss your
                art is for sale & i'm buying

LAVINIA: keep your well-spoken hands off
me you make me sick with your mouth's stench
stuffed with power yes i'm for sale
my life this small barely
lived but loved life i've
paid a lot for it & i've cheated myself
out of it for someone who bought me
a home my love paid it off dollar
for dollar the forever enticing
beautiful doll face that costs nothing
except a life that's cheap
for anyone who can
pay

1ST JOHN: yeah so what's all the fuss as long as i
pay & not pretend with fake bills i
pay cash in your hand & something
extra for the pleasing look of
contradiction your poetry is really
worth its price come on
let's get it on with your
poetry

LAVINIA: screw your wordiness go play with
yourself the stuff you sell as poetry
you can't buy from me
illiterates can't deal in this
old art the word order
will surely give you too hard
a time judging from your big
talk whose exclamation points
are always missing at the end go on
leave

1ST JOHN: lavinia your tongue will soon be free
                       like a butterfly free
                       your hands like two wings free
                       lavinia they will be free
                       your tongue speaking free
                       your hands lifted against
                       everyone free
                       lavinia you too will be free
                       like wild game

he exits.

LAVINIA: titus

TITUS: *silent*

LAVINIA: once hunters now we are the
                       hunted & hound with heckling
                       tongues the happiness left
                       behind just like booty which
                       we ourselves now are for the dogs
                       who already for a long time have been
                       sniffing our blood with their fighting mugs
                       their chops already trembling
                       anticipating the joy of their catch
                       a huntsman's luck thanks to us
                       when they bury their bloody
                       hands into the wounds
                       of our bodies

                       titus my noble protector
                       for whom i couldn't blow the hunting
                       horn enough for his
                       pursuit of all things that do creep
                       & fly & still have a mouth to

breathe out of which a
perhaps hostile gentle
breeze could blow that
takes from caesar what belongs
to caesar what remains
for the all-too-mortal like us
the final reasons
titus surely remain for us it may
be enough for the hunter
who believes his posthumous fame
is a trophy for the wall
it's not enough for me to
live & live is what i want titus
but only fear lives in
me & you surely you aren't
hearing my complaint oh
my titus noble protector
keep your ears shut before
the great hunting cry

2ND JOHN: lavinia —
look at the fine artists
a whore today has public
dealings & spreads her legs
for the people doing street art how
is it that your iron
curtain is now open
to the masses

LAVINIA: keep your loathsome hands off
me titus protect me from the
rabble leave me alone keep your
hands off me don't leave me
alone with them titus

2ND JOHN: why all the fuss you're
offering yourself & i'm
inquiring & don't you
still wonder too if
you like standing there your
freewheeling john is so free & giving
& has a hankering for the sweet
fruits the kind that are being
offered for sale i'm not
stealing there won't be a kiss
that i won't pay for nothing
caught between
my teeth that won't
have exchange value in the hands
of a merchant still
i pay for the good time
here titus cash in
your hand it's the price
you get
with your muse & now
come quick perishable
is the love that you give

LAVINIA: i'll go with whomever i
please and with you
never in my life

2ND JOHN: yeah lavinia your life will get
its days & they will be bloody
& you will not prevent yourself
from wishing to have what you have
held from me so prudishly even the
blood between your teeth will
not make your body clean
of the guilt & fear with a

roman in your belly standing
in the gutter that which you receive
will quickly be all the more painful
lavinia sweetly enjoy your
days among them already broods
pompey in his pride & the pleasure
suddenly interrupted during the loveplay
of descent hail titus has left
you the voice you
will still need it for two

LAVINIA: have they cut out your tongue because of
the poet's oracle have they banished
the bird flight because of the eyes
peering behind a
curtain made of night look out
titus
i stood like a venus
caught in rome's eye unreachable
for the poor whose eyes hid their
open lust behind
holy timidity inviolable i
was a statue spellbound within the
delicate game of limbs a
still statue moves by the
fingertips of zeus a
stone with veins of blood & for the
heart of the gods they could not
bear the beauty
not the mirror which still is full of
arrivals just as their mirror
image was now each person ought
to see me as the mirror
of his pleasures & lay his ear upon
my breast & it is not

my heartbeat that he might
feel & doesn't want to know
if a stone has a heart if
a stone has a heart for the one
whose heart turns to stone again
beneath all the hands of the
torso it was again

after a despairingly tender attempt to resuscitate the statue of titus, lavinia smashes it to pieces. darkness.

Translated from the German by John Hamilton

8

(e.) TWIN GABRIEL

MANFRED PERNICE

A.R. PENCK

ANDREAS KOCH

BETTINA ALLAMODA

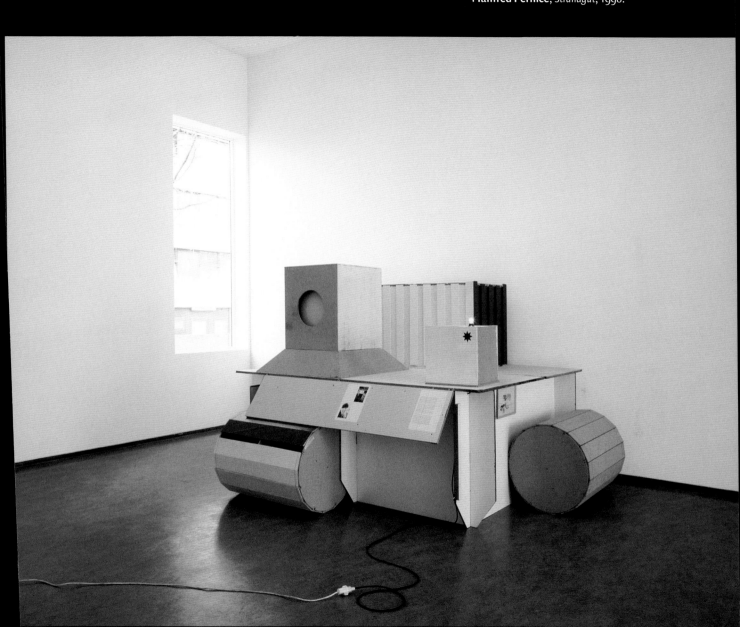

LEFT:
A. R. Penck, *Standart Model*, 1973.

BELOW:
Andreas Koch, (left) *Module*, 1995.
(right) *Wolkenkratzer (Skyscraper)*, 1995.

Bettina Allamoda, *Retina Room*, 1996–1998.

BETTINA ALLAMODA

Les artistes decorateurs

The materials for the multipiece work *Les artistes decorateurs* were salvaged from the Optical Museum of Jena after the fall of the Berlin Wall. When the museum, which had originally been designed for the German Democratic Republic, was refurbished in 1994, Bettina Allamoda recycled parts of the 1978 interior as found objects and made individual pieces that could be installed in almost any space. Based on sixties-era French habitat modules, these pieces reconstituted and refunctionalized space-defining objects from the Jena museum, such as vitrines, corresponding wall mural sections, and even the carpeting of the museum's former "Micro Room." The basic material was neither refurbished nor restored, but taken from an alien and inaccessible past and set into a new frame of perception.

(e.) TWIN GABRIEL: ON MAN AND SNAILS

Since 1990 the art duo Else Gabriel and Ullf Wrede have examined the blurred border between fact and fiction, working under the concept of "plastic planning," in which works of art are models with rules in constant flux. In December of 1996 the artists released five thousand snails inside a museum, to demonstrate the complex behaviors of simple organisms—as hermaphroditic creatures, the mollusks have a highly changeable sex life and continually redefine criteria for social relations.

(e.) Twin Gabriel's interest in mutability and contradiction has an autobiographical source, formed in part by their life in the German Democratic Republic. Faced with the system of state control, the artists created their own second, unofficial identity. Autonomous laws and their failures are an essential part of (e.) Twin Gabriel's work. The video and photo installation *Belle indifférence* combined images of Else Gabriel's pregnancy with scenes from a London civil chamber. The video showed a trip through various tunnels accompanied by uninterrupted screaming—rage, enthusiasm, or perhaps the panic before giving birth. In the photos, the very pregnant artist posed in her bathrobe in front of hospitals and airports. By modeling her restriction of free movement opposite urban codes, Gabriel made visible the paradoxical relationship between life and the big city.

In another project, (e) Twin Gabriel invented a few thousand identities whose names were taken from an old German lexicon and continually rearranged in installation pieces. In 1997, at the Neue Berliner Kunstverein, an exhibition of large-format computer prints was mounted, documenting an anonymous private scrapbook derived from two folios that the duo had purchased at a flea market. As artists, (e.) Twin Gabriel simply make experience possible—then the work takes on a narrative of its own.

Harald Fricke

Translated from the German by John Hamilton

RETURN
TO BERLIN
CEES NOOTEBOOM

IN MAY OF 1997 I WAS at Loyola Marymount University in Los Angeles, for the ceremonial unveiling of a piece of the Berlin Wall. Given to the university by the city of Berlin, the historical object stood there like an orphan without an orphanage, shy and even a bit forlorn. It bore a declaration of love for a certain Kristin, surrounded by childish paintings in cheerful colors. Students stood around the speakers in a large circle, listening raptly to the unimpeachable vocabulary rolling across the green lawn. Oppression and Freedom, Struggle and History; abstractions that seemed to have as much to do with the piece of cement we celebrated here as the two sparrows that briefly landed on it, with the innocence of creatures permitted to live outside of human history.

It was a sunny day, and the ocean tempered the heat of the nearby desert. I felt a bit strange as I drove there on one of the city's endless freeways. Just the word freeway, with all its associations, made thoughts and memories of the Wall grotesque. As the ceremony began I closed my eyes and tried to think of the first time I had seen the Wall, in the winter of 1963. In order to bring those days back, and put this piece of concrete back into the seamless wall from which it came, I called up images of men with dogs and guns, of watchtowers and searchlights. Only then was I twenty-nine again; only then was my own story anchored in history, and I not in the presence of this curious, ironic, postmodern detritus, which, and here precisely lies the irony, in its way belongs just as much to history.

Now, decades later and on the other side of the earth, I was observing the unveiling of a concrete object that would, presumably, remind people of a time that cannot and never will be summed up, if only because history has a Janus face that looks both to the past and, paradoxically, to the future. The future of yesterday had transformed the menace and the force that belonged to that piece of stone into harmless tourism.

On a recent trip to Berlin, I had the opportunity to reflect on my relationship to the city again. I tried to visit the Hotel Esplanade for sentimental reasons, but I could not find it. I came up out of the S-Bahn station at Potsdamer Platz and stepped into pandemonium. I was standing on what seemed to be a temporary bridge, which shook from the passage of heavy trucks. I didn't know where to look first. Far below me were swarms of workers busy with the foundations of Babylon or, God knows, a giant tunnel to Moscow—anything seemed possible. I leaned over the railing and watched something like a concrete grid being laid. Above me a forest of cranes transported black marble plates through the air. I could hear the ancient sound of iron on stone as I tried to make sense of the labyrinthine movements of the hundreds below. Who was directing it, I wondered, and how did all these people know exactly what to do? How did they find their way among the pipes, wires, and tubes? It seemed as if a giant city were rising out of the earth—as if it quite simply wanted to exist and were forging its path with an organic, unstoppable force. And while I felt a kind of euphoria, I also shivered because of the implications of the power visible here, a power that seemed to contradict the plaintive moaning and groaning that has risen from Germany recently. If this were no Potemkin city, then it simply had to be a vision of future strength.

A page was being turned, and with the thundering force of a pile driver. No fewer than three pasts were being buried in this magical landscape of orgiastic work, at the rate of a million images per second—trams, fashions, armies, bunkers, barricades, walls, police—all disappearing beneath the temples of the new power. I found myself standing before something that meant much more than what was visible at that moment. Somewhere, a few pathetic pieces of the Berlin Wall lay in a corner, like scenery shoved aside after a failed performance. Had it been an operetta? A Wagner opera in modern costume? A play by Heiner Müller? Or was it reality itself, the lingering shadow of which coincided with that other lonely piece of concrete I had seen presented in California?

In the distance I saw the wooden scaffolding of the new dome of the Reichstag, and then at last—absurd amid all this vigor—the Hotel Esplanade.

Instantly my memory shriveled. How could the hotel be so small? What had it looked like before? Now it stood strangely dwarfed by the towering new Sony building. I tried to imagine the Mercedes and BMWs that would eventually roll into the parking garages, the nouveaux riches amusing themselves in these new apartments according to the rituals of their era: spoiled by Filipino servant girls, with the soft murmur of the Dow Jones, Dax, and Nikkei in the background. But this was just as difficult as trying to imagine my own faded reality, when I had spent many long days in the Hotel Esplanade, with a lover who has since disappeared.

Not far from the hotel were the ruins of the Bayerische Hof, which was just being demolished back then. In my journal from those days I wrote: "Golden Germanic mosaics thunder down into the mud. Here lie the things that were part of something, but now no longer are. Abandoned toilet bowls, baths without faucets, faucets without baths, wineglasses from which no Breslauer, Nordhauser or Cottbuser will ever flow again. Everything—boots, prostitutes, waiters, menus, ashtrays, and trumpets—has been pulverized, crushed, and taken up to heaven, gone forever. In a small, modest café next door, two menus hang in the window. The year, 1940, stands above the descriptions of what a Messerschmidt pilot or recipient of the Iron Cross had eaten that day: Braised Veal Westmoreland, with Spinach and Potatoes. And did they drink the 1938 Niersteiner Spiegelberg with it, as is indicated? The café itself is closed, the chairs gather dust beneath the tables, as though the last clients had just left for the front, "but maybe," I wrote then, "they will come back and it will all begin again."

Now, more than thirty years later, I know that what begins again in Berlin will never be the same. Yet even now, the date on that menu—the unhappy year of 1940—sends me back to my own past. Although my life began seven years earlier, I cannot explain myself without thinking of 1940, if only because the war, which will only be over when everyone who still remembers something of it has died, seems to have erased the first seven years of my life, aided by something that I have only recently discovered. This brings me then to a pair of related digressions.

The first one has to do with being a writer. There is a famous literary controversy between the novelist Marcel Proust and the critic and essayist Charles-Augustin Sainte-Beuve, which comes down to this: Sainte-Beuve believed that one ought to know as much as possible about the life of a writer, while Proust believed that nothing but the author's books mattered. He also believed that writers and poets never truly reveal themselves in conversation, so that an author's conversations mean nothing compared to his writing, in which he draws from a much deeper layer of his personality, traveling around like an explorer, bringing back things that must not be wasted in a superficial conversation. I cannot compare myself to Proust, of course, but in this regard I am a respectable Proustian. In the shamelessly exhibitionist culture in which we live, where private life is played out in the public sphere and writers become their own public personas, the hidden kernel is no longer mysteriously conveyed by means of the miraculous and holy lies of fiction, but flows unfermented from the glass screen to thousands of people who will never read their books. In short, I think that people can only talk about themselves in a very limited way.

The second digression concerns the peculiar inadequacy of my own memory. Nabokov could command his memory to speak—*Speak, Memory* is an imperative, after all, or at least an entreaty formulated in the imperative. But for me such a command has no effect; my memory simply doesn't reply. Augustine likewise writes of the palace of memory, in which one can discover all sorts of treasures. But for me that palace is always closed. Scraps, shadows, and fragments are all I can perceive behind the dirty or broken windows of my palazzo, which seems to exist in a permanent twilight.

I have always thought, perhaps primitively, that my absence of memory was a result of the thundering clap of the first day of the war, a numbing that stretched forward as well as backward, a hole into which children's books, friends, and teachers have namelessly disappeared. But not long ago I realized that its causes may be more than the bomber planes of those first days, more than the picture of Rotterdam burning on the distant horizon. Recently an exhibition on my life and work opened in The Hague, where I was born in 1933. This included, much to my dislike, a rather comprehensive examination of my past. The research was conducted by a very thorough person, who suggested that in the years of crisis before the war, my family moved no fewer than seven times within the city. My mother, who is still alive, denied this fiercely at the time, but had to admit defeat when confronted with records from the city register. After that came the war years, chaos, the divorce of my parents, evacuation, a hungry winter, the death of my father during an English bombardment— surely enough to barricade a palace. Only later, when I had gained a certain power over my life, did I add a wing to which I have access. Otherwise both life and writing would have been impossible. The main building, however, remains closed. Never will I be able, like Borges, to tell you which books I read in my father's library, or, like Proust, to recount long conversations with my grandmother, or, like Nabokov, to cheerfully disclose the idiosyncrasies of my French governess. This is not only because my father did not have a library, or because both my grandmothers died before I could know them, or because the nanny ran off with my father in the middle of the war, but above all because something was radically and permanently erased by an annihilating power from outside, leaving me empty-handed, but with a fascination for the past—for disappearance, transience, memoirs, ruins, and antiquity—for everything, in short, that is suggested by the word "history."

I provide this history—for even these personal stories that are only a very small part of an era can be called history—in order to explain why Berlin has fascinated me for so long. I have the sense that what happened to me happened in Berlin, but on an infinitely greater scale and with far more gruesome consequences. The ruins, voids, and holes I encountered on my very first visit were trying to tell me something that I did not really understand at the time, namely *nothing*. The word annihilation contains *nihil*—Latin for nothing—and all these absences in this annihilated city were the result, we must remember, of a man who wrote a book in the twenties, in which a clear and lucid program for the annihilation of an entire people was articulated. This is why I find The Jewish Museum in Berlin, designed by Daniel Libeskind, to be so profoundly moving. For Libeskind designed this museum to evoke that nothing. To express the presence of absence is something only art can do, but the

nothingness receives its weight precisely from that which is *not* there—which, of course, once *was* there.

The fifties and the early sixties were perhaps not the most appealing years to be young. When I visited Berlin for the first time, the city looked like an orgy of annihilation, the night after the dance of the dead. It still tasted like war, and seemed like a continuation of what I had seen and heard as a child. At the same time, though, a new element had been added—a fissure that ran through the world but was more visible here than anywhere else, as if it were again up to Berlin to make something clear to the world. Two social and political philosophies were being implemented separately, and in one oddly divided language. That I made my journey with two older friends who had both been in Dachau contributed to the apocalyptic quality of that first visit. I found myself in a confusing tangle of feelings and experiences, which were tempered by the cynical camp humor of my friends, and the amazing way they had of dealing with memories.

I may have been able to feel all this when I was first in Berlin, but I couldn't think it yet. I was too busy with the rest of the world. The Netherlands, like Germany, was a place without color in those years. I remember them almost entirely in gray. My first journeys, which I embarked on when I was eighteen or so, were to the North, and it was while returning from one of them that I passed through Germany for the first time. The scraps provided by my inadequate recollections include impassable roads, city neighborhoods entirely devastated, and the indomitable but equally unimaginative uniformity of reconstruction. And if I focus more sharply I can see and hear an abandoned, nocturnal train yard, filled with shunting locomotives, where I took dramatic leave of someone while a voice from the loudspeaker made announcements in a language to which I had not yet grown accustomed, one that did not want to be the same language as the poems by Goethe and Rilke I had read in school.

In 1989, I was invited by the German Academic Exchange Service (DAAD) to spend a year in Berlin, and I experienced everything that happened that year not as an incidental visitor, but as a resident of the city. While I may not have been German, I was very much a European, and it was not only a new country that was being forged there, but an entire continent. Events followed hard on one another that year. Gorbachev came to Berlin and gave Honecker a kiss that would seal the latter's fall, and his own not much later. A number of figures hurried across the stage in short-lived roles as statesmen. Currencies merged, and the two languages, which had to become one again, broke their teeth on each other. The euphoria faded and a strange union came into being, like a marriage of two people who became acquainted through a personal ad, but now cannot get rid of each other. A few generations were running the gauntlet through the chill of memory again, while some, who had been much more comfortable with just one past, stood by as if the word "union," which had stood like a holy emblem in their constitution, was never meant to become a reality. German students sometimes asked me at readings, "Aren't you afraid of us?" No, I wasn't afraid, but the fact that they seemed to think I should be, as if they still didn't trust their own country, did give me reason to think.

Recently I returned to Berlin, and then drove on to Leipzig and Halle. In the cathedral in Magdeburg and the Nicolaikirche in Leipzig there were two small exhibits. Once more I saw the ghostly images of the past—German soldiers executing German deserters, hanged partisans, and countless victims of bombing raids. There were also, however, photographs of the individuals who resisted, heroes and saints from ordinary life, people who never admitted defeat and who had paid for that with their lives. In Berlin I visited an exhibition titled "Images of Germany," which included hallucinatory works by Schönebeck and Baselitz, Kiefer and Loewig, Penck, and Immendorff, as well as the unforgettable *Self-Portrait with Jewish Identity Card* that Felix Nussbaum painted while hiding from the Nazis in Brussels, a year before his death. It is always art, in its greatness and sometimes also in its awkwardness, that prophesies, testifies, and remembers.

It is not a very long walk from the museum that now houses this work to Potsdamer Platz, and yet it seems very far. I do not know what the people standing there with me at the largest construction site in the world thought, but for me some words that I wrote in 1990, at the end of my *Berlin Notes*, came back to me: "I know that I have to take leave of this country-in-process, but I cannot do so yet. There are too many sentences and images still swirling in my thoughts. The German philosopher Johann Georg Hamann saw 'numbers, hidden signs, and hieroglyphs of God' in history. Whether they are from God or not I do not know, but after so many months I feel entangled in those signs. They are, as in Dresden or Potsdam, birthmarks on a living organism. Germany isn't finished. It is ancient, but is still being made, and it is just this that makes it fascinating."

I dedicated *Berlin Notes* to my friend, Willem Leonard Brugsma, who took me to Germany for the first time in the early sixties. As a young fighter in the resistance, Brugsma was arrested by the Gestapo in Paris, and had been in the camps at Natzweiler and Dachau for a number of years. He died recently, and at his funeral I remembered that first, heavily charged trip to Germany. This man, who could tell the most gruesome stories about his experiences in the camps, a big man who hadn't weighed much more than a hundred pounds when he was freed, was a passionate advocate for German unity; not, as one sometimes hears cynically, to make Germany less dangerous by binding it into Europe, but rather because he thought that one Germany belonged in one Europe. I mention that here because much of what one hears from Germany now is the sound of infinite weariness, a defeatist complaining. Suddenly German unification is no longer about ideas, but only about money. The original enthusiasm of the people is being subsumed by the demagogy of common sense.

This has always been a dangerous continent. It is solely responsible for the two ideologies that have made this century the most disastrous in history. I know that developing a Europe with one currency represents a large-scale, extremely complex political and economic maneuver for the continent, one that fills me with much fear. I also know that political unification limps behind it like an unhappy child, hindered by differences in language, ineradicable national ambitions, and an often invisible European parliament. But this is precisely where the challenge lies. If early European explorers had spent as much time calculating as those of today appear to, they would all have stayed home. But then a piece of the Berlin Wall would never have been in Los Angeles.

Translated from the Dutch by Duncan Dobbelmann

THE FASERSTOFF PROJEKT

GERRIT GOHLKE

Set in the countryside near Lake Fürstenberg, fifty miles north of Berlin, Ravensbrück was a concentration camp for women. It fell into the hands of the Soviet army after the war and remained closed to survivors and virtually unknown to the world until recently. It represents, therefore, two closed chapters of Germany's past. Ravensbrück, the camp, and Fürstenberg, a small city of old apartment buildings situated beside it, are two disconnected spheres that make up the *Faserstoff Projekt*, named after an industrial park at the camp where prisoners produced ammunition according to the doctrine "extermination by work." The *Faserstoff Projekt* was begun in 1994 by three curators: Peter Lang, Margi Miosga, and Christoph Tannert. Since 1995, when the first artists met with survivors, forty-six artists have developed proposals for installations at the Ravensbrück site.

There has been enormous controversy in Berlin over the creation of a memorial for Europe's murdered Jews. In reaction, the *Faserstoff Projekt* attempts to deal with history, not as something abstracted into an object of pathos or guarded conservatively in museums, but as an ongoing dialogue with the present. The project deals not only with the concept of a memorial and its inherent efficiency, but also with the painful attempts that have taken place to transform the area around the former camp from a no-man's-land into a structure intended to sustain normal life (in 1991, Ravensbrück barely escaped being transformed into a shopping mall and parking garage).

The project is supplemented by an Internet site that shows the individual proposals as works in progress and documents the artists' own changing relationships to the past. The artworks will be temporarily installed in the Faserstoff area by the year 2000 (temporarily, so that the aesthetic examination of the past will not become a formula for memory). If the *Faserstoff Projekt* comes to be regarded as the clear opponent of monument culture, the project will have reached its objective.

KARL-HARTMUT LERCH AND HERMANN KLEINKNECHT: THE MECHANICS OF MEMORY

From a growing collection of amateur films on Germany's recent history, Lerch and Kleinknecht attempt to create a cross-section of the collective visual memory. Material was gathered throughout Europe and includes American Signal Corps footage, witness accounts of Nazi war crimes, and documentation of Nazi terror and the fall of Hitler's regime. Gaps in the visual record were supplemented with oral accounts added after the footage was compiled, showing how images used to formulate personal histories can serve to deceive individuals about past events.

At the film's core is a section whose title, *Screen Memory*, is borrowed from Freud. It refers to the phenomenon when an event actually experienced is replaced in the mind by something imagined. Here the artists set single scenes against one other in an associative manner. But beyond the selection of the image combinations no position is drawn, no didactic statement sought. In this way, Lerch and Kleinknecht display the dilemmas of history before our eyes.

Andreas Strobel

In all of her work, Rivka Rinn is concerned with the essence of writing and how it transcends the limits of space and time. This function of language is especially clear and affecting in the six-part photo piece *Time Station*, which Rivka Rinn has dedicated to Milena Jesenska (1896–1944). A journalist from Prague, Jesenska was known primarily as a friend of Franz Kafka's. She met Kafka in 1920 in Vienna through her first husband, the writer Ernst Polak, and became Kafka's first translator. The correspondence between Jesenska and Kafka has been compiled into the book *Letters to Milena*.

After her divorce from Polak, Jesenska returned to Prague where she was involved with the Communist Party and became a member of the Czech avant-garde. After Hitler's occupation in February of 1939, she helped Jewish and Czech peasants flee the country. She worked underground as an editor for an illegal magazine, calling for opposition against the occupying army. In 1940 she was arrested by the Gestapo and taken to Ravensbrück where she died in 1944.

Another witness and former prisoner with Milena in Ravensbrück, Hannah Semer, provided Rinn with important information for her memorial project. Semer, who was seventeen at the time, recalled the survival strategies women in the camp developed in response to their life of degradation and torture. These women of different nationalities collected poems, songs, drawings, and caricatures, recorded them on stolen paper, and bound them into books that were kept hidden in a large box. A favorite technique for enduring hunger was sharing memories of cooking recipes. Rinn has taken some of these recipes and juxtaposed them with her repertoire of speed-snapshots, in an attempt to construct a forum for memory. As Semer recounted, they were recipes for dishes that were especially rich and caloric, like Black Forest cherry torte and Esterhazy cream pie. These recipes were collected in a book called the *Songbook of the Hungry*, bound in a piece of blue velvet that one of the inmates had stolen from the SS private tailor shop—fabric meant for a ball gown for the wife of one of the guards.

Christa Steinle

ERIK STEINBRECHER

Erik Steinbrecher works with photographic images, constructed and also found objects. He presents photographic motifs that challenge the viewer with their potential for questions (How does everyday fascism manifest itself today?). In Steinbrecher's image series, one encounters the unfamiliar in the familiar and is given the opportunity to rid oneself of the constraints of day-to-day common sense. There is nothing unambiguous in the images: an anonymous body, a furnished living room, body parts, flowers, a rumpled bed-sheet, the buttress of a barbed wire fence . . .

It is becoming more and more difficult to pose questions in terms of right and wrong, good and bad, idylls and ghettos, victims and perpetrators. A consensus as to the significance of failure has widely disappeared from the German political consciousness, as politics and morality wash over a contradictory life. In this context, Steinbrecher's images demonstrate the relativism of opinions.

LOIS WEINBERGER

For Lois Weinberger, poetry lies in the awareness that a catastrophic past anticipates future catastrophes. In an attempt to engage with the perspective of victims of the Ravensbrück camp, Weinberger has reconstructed a garden patch that camp victims secretly tended. The artist/gardener has lavished care and attention on his re-naturalized plot of herbs and vegetables. With his sturdy garden work he means to draw forth an almost invisible trace of memory, one that links the present with the past. As historical atrocities recede and then fade out, Weinberger's garden, fragile and alive in a world of concrete, subtly awakens us to the ever-present potentials for danger.

Christoph Tannert
Translated from the German by John Hamilton

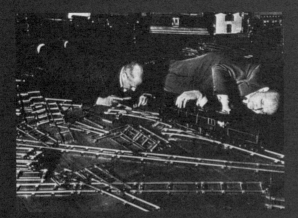

Alfred Eisenstædt, *Toy Train Society, Berlin, 1931.*

Aura Rosenberg plans to project videos shot at the children's park in Wuhlheide in former East Berlin, on the spot where the railroad tracks crossing the Faserstoff grounds at Ravensbrück are intersected by a wall.

Wuhlheide's Pioniereisenbahn, which opened in 1956, is a small yet fully functional railroad operated and maintained by children from nine to seventeen years old. An anniversary brochure for the railroad, which was modeled on those in Hungary and the Soviet Union, describes it in utopian terms: as harmony between Man, Nature, and Machine. It also stresses that the polytechnical training the Pioniereisenbahn offers was never intended to be militaristic; it was, instead, educational play. The long-standing ideal of socialism has been to abolish the division between work and leisure. If this goal has proven elusive, the example of children shows that it is not impossible; play is the means through which children learn to master the world.

In 1936 the German government laid railroad tracks for transporting artillery casings from the munitions factory at Ravensbrück. Formerly, this factory produced wicks for streetlamps. The tracks ran through the grounds of what would become the women's concentration camp at Ravensbrück. Later, women from the camp worked in the factory itself. One inmate, Ilse Stephan, described how prisoners had to load mountains of sharp steel tailings into wagons with their bloodied hands. Forced labor was a means of assimilating those who had been otherwise designated as useless. However, had efficiency really been the Nazis' aim, they could have issued gloves to the workers. Here, overturning the logic of work resulted in stultification—and ultimately genocide.

John Miller

225

GÜNTER KUNERT

The Jewish Cemetery in Weissensee

On granite slabs
fallen leaves. Under their touch
the gravestone sinks once more
into the earth: strangeland
that naturalizes only the dead
ruled by the silent vampires
oak yew and laurel.
With the passing seasons illegible
your name. No one
lifts the ivy above your uniqueness
any more out of curiosity.
For you have returned
to the enigma
that remains forever
motionless and hidden
beneath fickle impressions.

Translated from the German by Peter Constantine

9

FRANZ ACKERMANN

MARTIN KIPPENBERGER

NEO RAUCH

JÖRG IMMENDORFF

Franz Ackermann, *Untitled (Evasion XIII—5 Star Tropical)*, 1997.

Jörg Immendorff, *Café Deutschland III,* 1978.

HEINER MÜLLER

The Luckless Angel. Behind him the past silts up, pouring debris down on his wings and shoulders with a noise like buried drums, while in front of him the future becomes a growing mass, presses his eyes in, bursts his eyeballs like a star, the Word turns into a muffled gag, strangling him with his own breath. For a while the beat of his wings can still be seen, rockfalls heard in the din, subsiding before above behind him, the more violent their flailing the louder they are, sporadic now as they slow down. Then the moment closes over him: the luckless angel's resting place is this abrupt landfill of a place where he stands, waiting for history in the petrifaction of Flight Gaze Breath. Until the renewed noise of massive wingbeats propagates itself in waves through the stone and indicates his flight.
— circa 1958

I am the Angel of Perplexity. With my hands I distribute ecstasy, narcosis, oblivion, bodily lust, and agony. My conversation is silence, my song a scream. Horror lives in the shadow of my wings. My hope is the last breath. My hope is the first battle. I am the knife with which the dead man bursts open his coffin. I am he who will be. My flight is insurrection, my heaven the chasm of tomorrow.

—1979

The Luckless Angel 2

Between city and city
After the wall the sheer fall
Wind at the shoulders the alien
Hand on solitary flesh
The angel I can still hear him
But his face is no more than
Yours that I don't know

—1991

Yesterday on a Sunny Afternoon

As I drove through the dead city of Berlin
Returning home from some foreign country
I felt for the first time the need
To disinter my wife from her cemetery plot
Two full shovels I'd heaped on her myself
And see what still remained of her
Bones I'd never seen while she was alive
To hold her skull in my hand
And picture what her face was like
Behind the masks she wore
Through the dead city of Berlin and other cities
When her skull was clothed with her flesh.

I didn't yield to this need
Because I was afraid of the police and the talk of my friends.

Fremder Blick: Farewell to Berlin

From my cell in front of the blank copy
In my head a drama for an empty auditorium
Deaf are the victors the vanquished dumb
A strange look at a strange city
Yellow-gray clouds drift past the windowpane
Gray-white pigeons are shitting on Berlin

December 14, 1994

Translated from the German by Iain Bamforth

WAR WITHOUT BATTLE: FROM THE AUTOBIOGRAPHY

HEINER MÜLLER

Heiner Müller was, without doubt, the most important playwright since Bertolt Brecht to live and work in Berlin. By the time Müller died in 1995, at the age of sixty-six, he had formally inherited Brecht's mantle. He was running the Berliner Ensemble, the company Brecht founded with Helene Weigel. He had outwitted, exhausted, and driven off his rivals. And his word at the theater was law, though some critics maintained that the only truly inspired decision of his brief tenure was to restore the caviar and smoked salmon served in the company's dining room during the last decades of the German Democratic Republic, thus sparing himself the bourgeois capitalist cafeteria food of the united Germany.

It seems there was no one Heiner Müller. He had the fatal German disease called Innerlichkeit—"innerness"—but his cynicism was pure Berlin. He was a man of almost tragic gloom and at the same time spectacular mundanity. His plays could be leaden with meaning, but his conversation was dry, ironic, and amused. He was a passionate socialist who practiced the realpolitik of a seasoned commissar. He lived in East Berlin, but earned his fame, his money, and his privilege on the far side of the Wall, along with a liberty not shared by ordinary East Germans. He relished the pleasures of the capitalist West that he claimed to despise. The price he paid was his compliance with a regime that continued to ban a great deal of his own work.

Berliners on both sides of the Wall—even the wall in the head that exists now—adored Müller. He was a mirror of their fractured city, a trickster, a survivor, a dazzling contortionist of Germanness. They seemed to forgive him everything, even his dalliance with the East German secret police, the Stasi, with whom he talked occasionally in the 1980s in what he would later describe, smiling, as a harmless and even ameliorating exchange. It's a sign of the Berlin attitude that the novelist Christa Wolf, who was moralistic and pious when her own history as a Stasi informer was revealed, was never forgiven by Berliners. Müller was self-serving—he talked about his "right to cowardice in the face of the enemy" and never said who the enemy was—but he was neither moralistic nor pious, which is one reason Berlin embraced him. The city gave him a hero's funeral. He never pretended to be anyone but his several selves.

Jane Kramer

Childhood in Saxony

What are your very first memories?
The first is a trip to the cemetery with my grandmother. There was a monument for fallen soldiers
from World War I, made out of porphyry. It was an
enormous statue in the shape of a mother. For years
this war monument was connected in my mind to
a lilac image of Mother, laden with anxiety, and
perhaps also to my grandmother, who took me to
the cemetery.

The second memory is of a time when my
parents and I were sick. All three of us were in bed.
A nurse, probably from a church organization,
came to see us regularly, and one time she brought
us strawberries. These strawberries were my first
experience of happiness.

Then the arrest of my father in 1933. I had a
small room of my own, and was lying there in bed.
It was rather early in the morning, around five or
six. I woke to the sound of voices and commotion in
the room next to mine. There were men in SA
uniforms throwing books on the floor, purging our
library of leftist literature. I could see through the
keyhole that my mother was standing beside them.
They were beating my father. I got back into bed and
closed my eyes. Then they were standing in the
doorway—the silhouettes of the two strapping SA

men, and between them the small figure of my father.
I pretended to be asleep, even when my father called
my name. . . .

We visited my father in a concentration camp. It
was a strikingly bleak landscape, and the camp was up
on a plateau. We had to talk to my father through the
mesh gate. He looked very thin and small. I showed
him pictures that I had made, and cigarette cards. My
mother couldn't bring herself to speak to him. Years
later, she told me that after seeing him I would call out
in my sleep, "Just jump over the fence!"

After he got out he told me a few stories about his
time inside. The first thing they did was shave a strip
right across the prisoners' heads. They called it "the
autobahn cut." Then they took mug shots, which
appeared in the local papers with captions saying,
"These are the Bolshevists who want to take away your
women, and the milk from your children." My father
had a somewhat yellowish complexion and black hair,
and at one roll call the commander, an SA captain,
asked him, "Jew?"

My father answered, "No, not that I know of."

"Then your mother was fucked by Jews."

My father's mother was an ardent National
Socialist; she adored Hitler because he didn't smoke,
didn't eat meat, and had no stories about women to
hide. My father told his mother this story later, of
course, and with a good deal of *Schadenfreude*.

What memories do you have of Eppendorf?

While my father was in the concentration camp there were a few boys, children of local officials, who told me that they could no longer play with me because my father was a criminal. This experience was an important harbinger of much that came later. I was always isolated, separated from the outside world at the very least by my invisibility. I did find a few friends, though. Once we were trying to destroy a swallow's nest in a cowshed by throwing stones at it. In order to get some attention, I took particularly careful aim, and hit the nest. Then I saw the young swallows lying on the ground. The farmer chased us from the cowshed. He had two somewhat slow sons, neither of whom had learned to read or write after six years in school. The older one went back into the barn with a flail and crushed the swallows. The brothers were rivals for the farm, their inheritance, and they fought all the time, sometimes with scythes. The younger one used to spur the dog on to chase us. We must have set records running away from that dog. Once he locked us in the corral and let the horses out.

What did books mean to you as a boy?

My father had a wonderful edition of Casanova's memoirs, with lusty color illustrations. Naturally, it was my favorite reading material. But he thought the book was too corrupting, at least for a boy my age. In any case, he exchanged the Casanova for editions of Schiller, Hebbel, and Körner. I read all of Schiller's plays, and all of Hebbel's as well. And from that point on I wanted to write plays. School couldn't ruin the classics for me because I already knew them. At the time I read a lot of paperbacks, because they were cheap and my father was constantly buying new ones. When I was twelve or thirteen I read the tales of Edgar Allan Poe. *The Narrative of Arthur Gordon Pym of Nantucket* was on my father's shelf, but he eventually took it away because there was a cannibalism scene in it. I had read it with particular interest because of that scene, of course. It made an unforgettable impression on me.

Wartime

In the fall of 1944, my school was shut down. Everyone was called up to assist in the war effort. Most of us simply had to report to the Work Service (*Reichsarbeitsdienst*). They were also looking for people for the SS, but initially they took only volunteers. That was the greatest fear, not just for me, but for everyone—that you might end up in the SS.

I remember the examination vaguely. No one wanted to join. We were fifteen years old. The whole class was scattered; no more than two or three of us went anywhere together. I had to report to the Work Service. Before the conscription there was a sort of guerrilla training, but I can't remember much about that time. They taught you things like how to use a bazooka, how to shoot, and how to find your way around in the woods. I couldn't shoot well, which was a great stroke of luck. I saw poorly without my glasses. For years I hadn't been able to read a thing on the blackboard. That was my salvation.

The Work Service had nothing to do with work, of course. The most important thing was the shooting. The instructor was fairly young, in his mid-twenties; an idealistic Nazi and a principled man. He split us up into "men" and "idiots," based on the shooting results. I was an idiot, and the idiots didn't interest him. The training didn't last very long at any rate, not more than a few weeks. By then the Russians were in Mecklenburg. Our instructors preferred capture by the Americans to capture by the Russians, and so we marched westward to Schwerin. At some point, roughly halfway there, a messenger on a motorcycle approached from the front, stopped briefly, and quickly rode on past us. Then our instructor, sobbing like a child, walked along the column saying, "The Führer has fallen."

A few hours later we stopped at a large farm that had been abandoned, and the commander, whom we had hardly seen, delivered a speech. The Führer had fallen, and the band of traitors surrounding Dönitz had capitulated. He was no longer in a position to give us orders, but those among us who were real men and Germans could head into the woods with him to continue the fight. The others could go home. Five or six German men joined him, and together they struck out for the bush. The rest of us scattered into the countryside and trotted along on our own, rather relieved. . . .

The end of the war left me, quite suddenly, in a state of absolute freedom. I roamed through the countryside with no particular destination. I could hear shots now and then, as well as artillery, and could see tanks driving through cornfields in the distance. I came across a destroyed bridge; it was an image I have never forgotten. At one point I boarded a train traveling west, full of women, children, and soldiers. It continued on for a while, then stopped again. I heard shots and yelling. Then a few Russians with automatic pistols got on the train and searched it for soldiers. There was a pretty steep drop-off on one side. Two German soldiers said to me, "We're getting off here, want to come along?" So we scrambled down the slope. The Russians shot at us as we fled. There were dead horses lying around everywhere, and overturned wagons abandoned during a refugee trek. Next to one of the dead horses there was a bottle filled with homemade anise liqueur. It was the first anise liqueur I'd ever tasted. Then we ran into an

American soldier who stopped us. The first thing he did was take the bottle away from me. I have never forgiven the Americans for that.

I ended up in a paddock—a cattle paddock—in American captivity. New prisoners arrived constantly, and there was nothing to eat. The Americans were very anxious. As evening approached they drove us, in columns, toward Schwerin. Every five meters along the road there stood a heavily armed American soldier. If anyone stepped to the side, even to pee, the guards would shoot immediately. You could see the effects of the propaganda on them: they thought the Germans were beasts, dangerous savages.

Before being captured I had found a can of meat somewhere. I exchanged it with someone across the fence for a civilian jacket. It was dark gray with light stripes, and rather tattered and torn. There was a guard at the gate, a husky American. I waited for two days, and then went up and talked with him. I asked him where he was from—Iowa—if he had a family, if he had a wife and kids. He had two kids, and he showed me photos. I said, "Beautiful kids, beautiful family." Then we shook hands and he let me leave. Just like that I was outside. It didn't take any particular cunning. I was sixteen.

I made a big detour around Schwerin and arrived in a village, where I stayed for a few weeks. Some former concentration camp prisoners had taken shelter in barns there. There were Italians, Poles, and a Romanian who had been with the circus and knew a lot about horses. A gypsy read my palm and foretold that I would be taken to Siberia with an older man, if I went to the East. I couldn't get rid of her; she followed me everywhere. The Italian refugees butchered calves in the meadows near the village. The farmers would come out with clubs, yelling, but they were outnumbered. There was no justice. We ate the veal out in front of the barn. After the calves it was the horses' turn. They tasted good, too, but they had to be roasted quickly. The Romanian knew that.

Eventually we had even run out of horses. We heard that in a neighboring barn there were Poles brewing schnapps. They had found a canister of spirits and mixed it with a brownish drink of deadly intensity. The important part was that they gave you a piece of bacon and a piece of bread if you drank with them; essentially we submitted to the schnapps ceremony out of physical necessity. For some reason I took a blow to the chin from one of the Poles and woke up some twelve hours later beside a cesspool. I probably said something about the schnapps, but I don't remember. I had never had schnapps before. We were a multicultural society, in a state of total anarchy.

The Early Years in Berlin

I was in Berlin for the first time when the war ended. I went on one of the early trains from Waren to Saxony. It ran in small stretches from Schwerin through Berlin to Wittenberg, I think. My first image of Berlin was the Anhalter railway station in 1946; parts of the old building were still standing. I rode in a coal car, along with a former teacher from my school in Waren. He was from Berlin originally and was returning for the first time since the war had begun. This man, who was helpless on the coal car, had taught me French for the first two days of the term, before I was called up. He had spent those classes telling us stories about the cavalry in the First World War. Now I had to make sure he didn't fall off the train. He gave me a lecture about how I must be a mathematical genius because of my physiognomy. In any case, I succeeded in keeping him on the coal heap. I think I spent the night at his place in Berlin. The trains were few and far between, and I also passed two or three days in Wilmersdorf. I even met a writer there. He called himself Müller-Osten, and he struck a highly curious figure at the typewriter. Müller-Osten on his old typewriter and the bombed-out Anhalter Bahnhof—that was Berlin.

Aside from writing, my efforts were consistently directed at somehow finding money or work. I knew what I wanted to write, but no one was buying that kind of work. I came to know some editors, including Hanna-Heide K. One time I sat with her in a room in the Adlon and admired her breasts. She had the loveliest breasts in Berlin—in my circle, in any case. But it never went further than that. I often had all-night conversations with her. She was a producer of kitsch, who wrote novels and poems with ridiculous titles. For example: *I sit at the typewriter / What do I type for / For Korea / I sit at the sewing machine*, and so on.

I had learned in Saxony that if you see a girl you like, you chat her up. And so that is exactly what I did in the train station on Friedrichstrasse. I tried to chat up a girl who looked good to me, and she said, "Get a clue." That was Berlin for me.

At the time you clearly supported the young German Democratic Republic.
My support for the GDR had to do with Brecht. Aside from Brecht there were hardly any writers in the GDR who held any significance for me, but he legitimized support for the system. That was very important. Proof of its superiority lay in the fact that its literature—Brecht, Seghers, Sholokov, Mayakovsky— was better. I never thought about leaving. My support had nothing to do with whether socialism could win the day in the GDR. That is more a practical or political consideration. Brecht was an example of the fact that one could be an artist and a communist—

with or without, against or in spite of the system. He represented a European position as opposed to a national one. And naturally, for dramatists a dictatorship is far more colorful than a democracy. Shakespeare would be inconceivable in a democracy. Living in the GDR meant, above all, living amid rich material. It is the same thing with architecture. Architecture has more to do with the state than painting does, and drama has more to do with the state than other forms of literature. Drama has a specific relationship with power; it involves resistance to power and a fascination with—even a desire to participate in—power. Perhaps one submits to power in order to participate in it. And what has happened in my texts over the course of the years has less to do with me than with a reaction to the deterioration of power. In the end there was only a vacuum, and it is that to which the texts reacted. The work becomes a search for a power that can still be contested.

Did you have any relations with Brecht?
The first play I saw by Brecht was *Mother Courage*. It must have been between 1949 and 1951. I had already read the Surrealists and American literature (Hemingway, Faulkner)—I knew all of that before I encountered Brecht's work. After Sartre and Anouilh it seemed very gray and dry. Then I read *Roundheads and Peakheads* in a magazine. That was somewhat more interesting. Although the *Courage* production in Berlin didn't make a strong impression on me, his work soon did, and eventually I had no goal but to belong to the Berliner Ensemble, and to work there. Fortunately it never happened. That it is fortunate is, of course, something I only learned much later.

I met Brecht twice. One time was at his house in Weissensee. We didn't talk, though. He had no

time, or else he had to leave. The fact that I went out there unannounced seems astonishing to me today, but when you're young you'll do anything. That would have been in 1951. The second time I went to see him at the Berliner Ensemble, and I showed him some poems. He looked through them and said, "Very interesting; and how do you support yourself?" I had expected this question, and had an answer ready: "I thought there might be some work here at the Berliner Ensemble for me." Then Brecht spoke the fatal sentence: "Go see Rülicke." That was his secretary. And so I went to see her. As soon as we met I knew she couldn't stand me, and I felt the same way about her. Brecht was allowed three master apprentices, and there were four applicants.

At that time the Berliner Ensemble was an island, a highly contested island. In Leipzig, for example, students at the theater institute had been expelled simply because they had seen Berliner Ensemble productions. Brecht was the Antichrist; he was poison. He had only been given the theater because the Russians had ordered it. He was deeply suspicious. Helene Weigel always claimed that a train full of students traveling from Leipzig to Berlin to see a production at the Berliner Ensemble had been intentionally derailed.

Rülicke asked me to write up a fable entitled "The Kremlin Glockenspiel." It was one of Brecht's projects. It was to be a masterpiece in which Lenin instructs a watchmaker to make the Kremlin chimes play a rendition of the "Communist International." In the end, the watchmaker is successful, and the "International" rings out. Stalin was to appear in it as well. Now and then Brecht had to do something for the functionaries; little gifts preserve a friendship. I wasn't able to produce the fable, and that was the end of that. Shortly afterwards, I wrote a play and submitted it to the Berliner Ensemble. A few weeks after I had sent it in I overheard a conversation about this play in the restaurant at the Deutsche Theater. People were saying that there was only room for the best at the Berliner Ensemble, which meant that I unfortunately didn't belong there.

What was your life in Berlin like at the time?
Nomadic. The biggest problem was that I had no income, apartment, or residence permit. To get a residence or a moving permit, you had to have work in Berlin, and to get work you needed a residence permit. It was the usual vicious circle of bureaucracy.

The best way to get information on what was really going on in Germany was by visiting the bars. That was the belly of Berlin: in bars you get to know all kinds of people, and in an entirely unique way. Part of the GDR's political strategy involved getting rid of the bars, and they were eventually leveled and turned into cafés, which were controllable and no longer proletarian. The proletariat and the youth, those were the archenemies of the state. Proletarian Berlin was demolished by the great building projects of the United Socialist Party of Germany (SED). It was an attempt to restore Wilhelmian Berlin, the city as it had been before the First World War, but in plastic; it had to do with repressing what had happened from 1933 to 1945. And so the proletarian milieu was liquidated.

I went to bars quite often, and I often stayed there overnight. You could always sleep in the Mitropa in the train station on Friedrichstrasse, which was open all the time, if you had money for a beer. You could bring bread for yourself, and sleep after you drank your beer, with your head on the table. The late shift ended at two in the morning and the next shift didn't begin until four. When the shifts changed they took the chair out from under

your ass. When the morning shift arrived, you needed to have money for another beer; if you did, you could stay there, and go back to sleep. That was really a good time, the prime time for gathering material.

Later I often went to the Café Nord. It was a typical dive, open all night, on the corner of Schönhauser and Wiechertstrasse. It still exists, but since then it has been spruced up and now is more like a disco with doormen. One night I heard a story from a Stalingrad soldier that went word for word into my play, *Germania Death in Berlin*. I didn't add anything to his account. He was drunk when he came in; the bartender wouldn't serve him any more, and he sat down next to me. Then I ordered something and he started telling this story. Even the part about the undersecretary is from him—he met him later in the GDR. The undersecretary had served with him in Stalingrad and could still crawl. Word for word: "Can you still crawl, Willy, you old pig?" You can't invent something like that. Or at least I couldn't have invented it.

East Berlin in the Seventies

What was it that interested you about modern German history?
When you see that the tree no longer produces fruit, that it has begun to rot, you check the roots. During these years the stagnation in the GDR was complete. But then everything buried down below rises to the surface. There was no longer any forward momentum, just various measures of restraint and fortification as the GDR approached its inevitable end, a by-product of the Soviet decline. I didn't know it at the time, I only described it; the text knows more than the author.

When did you first encounter Shakespeare?
When we began to read English in school I borrowed

an annotated English edition of *Hamlet* from the school library. I understood almost nothing, naturally, but I read it again and again. At a certain stage it is good to read texts in a language you don't quite understand. You learn a lot more than you do when you understand everything. That way you approach the thing from below, from the cellar. For me, Shakespeare was the antidote to Brecht, to the simplification in Brecht, which is the quality that most of those who worked with Brecht succumbed to. Shakespeare is not simple, but he is also not calculated. There is always an extraordinarily complex organic structure in his plays. I remember the first time I felt this clearly, when I read *Richard III*. The play as body, where the motion of this body is the play, an animalistic motion. It was exactly the same with the translation of *As You Like It*. A sensual experience . . . That suppleness can't be found in Brecht. Compared to that what Brecht did was Bavarian folk dancing.

And the most important play for you?
I'm afraid the most important play for me is *Hamlet*; probably because it was the first thing by Shakespeare I tried to read, and because it has the most to do with me, and with Germany. For the English, *Hamlet* is perhaps not an important play at all, or, as T.S. Eliot suggested, perhaps simply a failed one. But for us, *Hamlet* is interesting precisely because Shakespeare tries to express something he doesn't have command over, an experience he can't grasp. In Germany you can produce *Hamlet* with idiots and people will still go to see it.

Shakespeare had meaning for you in relation to the GDR?
Germany provided great material for drama, until reunification. I'm afraid it is quite possible that the end of the reception of Shakespeare in Germany has

come with the end of the GDR. I don't know why Shakespeare would be produced in the Federal Republic now, except for the comedies. Perhaps the time has finally come for Molière. But Shakespeare will not disappear, of course; the state is on the rise again. The more state, the more Shakespeare. In New York, in 1986, at the production of my *Hamletmachine* directed by Robert Wilson, this connection between theater and reality—as in Shakespeare's time—caught my attention. The simple fact that many people came to the theater by subway was striking. Giordano Bruno describes a trip to the Globe Theater in London: how you were attacked on every second corner, or fell into an excavation every third corner.

The End of the GDR

What sort of memories do you have of the last years before the end of the GDR?
There was always a reassuring argument, the wait for "the biological solution," the hope that Honecker would die along with a few of the others. . . . But the problem was that the situation could only be changed by the collapse of the entire system, a system that had essentially been sentenced to death—at least economically—since 1918. I waited for the decline, but didn't contribute to it.

The problem from my perspective was the complete absence of alternatives. Every Pole is first a Pole, and the difference between communists and dissidents changes absolutely nothing about that. The identity of the Germans was and is the Deutsche mark. Taking the mark away from the GDR population meant taking away their identity. Poles could dream of another Poland, but for East Germans there was no alternative to the Federal Republic. Only now, after reunification, is there a foundation for class struggle in Germany again. Now nothing more can be transferred to the enemy. Now, although it will surely take some time, social contradictions can develop, free of ideologies. The exultation of some German intellectuals over the Gulf War, the quiescent glee over a new Hitler in the guise of Saddam Hussein, betrays an anxiety produced by the prospect of life without an enemy. The condemnation of the GDR and the demonization of its security apparatus not only express the usual anticommunist sentiments but also anaesthetize these anxieties. When you no longer have an enemy you find it in the mirror.

What do you think now, at the outset of 1992, of this disappearing state?
For an author it is a privilege to have seen the fall of three states in one lifetime; the Weimar Republic, the fascist state, and the GDR. Surely, however, I will not see the fall of the Federal Republic.

★ ★ ★

The first edition of Heiner Müller's autobiography, War without Battle, was published in 1992. In early 1993, when his Stasi files were released along with those of thousands of other citizens, Müller was publicly criticized for not having addressed his involvement with the Stasi in the book. Later in 1993, a second edition of the book appeared, which included additional questions and answers, as well as copies of all the relevant documents. The following exchanges with journalist Thomas Assheuer were among the material added to the second edition.

The Human Right to Cowardice

Since the end of the GDR the West German press has been very critical of certain East German intellectuals' involvement with the Stasi. First it was Sascha Anderson, then Christa Wolf, and then one day the spotlight came to rest on a famous dramatist. You knew about it, but you were silent. Why?
What I knew was that I had had some conversations with the Stasi. I didn't write any reports, of course, nor was I ever asked to. They knew there were certain things they shouldn't try with me. On the other hand, there are many documents and scraps of paper with various vague plots and plans in the files. The officers had to produce some results, after all, even if it was nothing more than a pile of paper. At one point, for example, a grotesque plan came about to set me on two other writers, neither of whom I had any contact with. I was never even asked about it, but there it stands in my Stasi file. There is nothing about it in the files of these other writers. What astonished me most of all was the speed and nonchalance with which journalists began suggesting that I had spied on people or denounced them. Some of them even said I had received money for these things. It really did astonish me, how the whole thing happened.

But in your autobiography, you convey the impression that the Stasi just stopped by for a moment and smoked a Havana with you.

Unfortunately there was no Havana. At first I wanted something out of it also. The only problem was that what they wanted was quite different from what I wanted.

When did the Stasi first approach you, and what did they want from you?

It was in 1982, I think, and the meetings were very irregular. At times I talked to them once a year, then once every three or four months. They asked me about international politics, the dangers of nationalism, the Third World, and all kinds of things. Once I asked one of the agents why they were talking to me. It was never really clear. He said it was because they wanted me to stay.

I knew that I didn't have to talk to them. I wasn't blackmailed, I did it of my own volition. I thought I could get some help with concrete matters like visas and other things, and at times we even talked about cultural politics. I suppose I could be reproached for it. But why shouldn't I have tried to exert influence when I had the chance to do so? I never saw it as a moral dilemma.

And now people are saying that Heiner Müller was spying for the Stasi?

There isn't a shred of evidence to support this. What does exist is a list of the relationships the Stasi wanted to cultivate; this is how I was connected to the writers mentioned in my files. But they never actually asked me to help with these things; it was just for the files, so they had something they could show to their superiors. Many of my friends have looked through their own files since I was accused of spying, and no one discovered a thing. The fact is that there is nothing for them to discover. The controversy all goes back to the cliché that anyone who talked to the Stasi was a traitor and a pig.

So you wouldn't call this a form of collaboration? You must have had some sense of inner conflict.

What do you mean by "collaboration"? I wasn't for the dissolution of the GDR or for reunification. The conflict you suggest didn't exist at all, nor did I ever understand myself as a critic of the system in the sense you imply. The plays were simply realist. I don't consider myself responsible for the fact that the system couldn't endure this reality.

All the same though, it was a curious relationship between an intellectual and power.

I grew up with the feeling that I was suspect in the eyes of power. I have always felt like that, before and after 1945. From the perspective of the state I was always guilty.

As far as I'm concerned my integrity has not been soiled by my contacts with the Stasi, but I seem to be alone at the moment in this belief. I have lost a few friends, but they weren't friends anyway. It saves time.

And why didn't you write about all of this in your autobiography?

There is a human right to "cowardice in the face of the enemy," and I made use of it in that atmosphere. That the image of the enemy was accurate has been demonstrated nicely by these journalists.

Sometimes I get the sense that it would be difficult for you to write in a democracy.

There is no democracy anyhow. That too is a fiction. There has always been an oligarchy; democracy has never functioned any other way. There have always been a few living on the backs of many. Brecht formulated it politically. I'm not exactly celebrating the triumph of freedom and democracy.

Translated from the German by Daniel Slager

WOLF BIERMANN

I'm not so worried about Germany

I'm not so worried about Germany
Already on the path to unity
        'neath the billionfold rain
We're becoming pretty wet but not the same
Freedom does hurt and makes a good game
        A curse it is, a blessing

        Nostalgia for the past will not do
        nor for the old concerns
        Germany Germany is once again one
        only I am split in two

I'm not so worried about Germany
The German wound is still a long way
        from being cured, and there flow
Streams of pain, where the scar is gaping
Now only black sap is bleeding
        not pouring out, but deep deep it goes

Nostalgia for the past will not do
nor for the old concerns
Germany Germany is once again one
only I am split in two

I'm not so worried about Germany
And as the world's child I'll enter the fray
        Among knowledge or belief
Among friend or foe, whether wife or man
The dear mother tongue can
        steal no fatherland and be a thief

Nostalgia for the past will not do
nor for the old concerns
Germany Germany is once again one
only I am split in two

Translated from the German by John Hamilton

CONTRIBUTORS

Franz Ackermann was born in 1963. He lives and works in Berlin.

Bettina Allamoda was born in Chicago in 1964. From 1983 to 1990 she studied at the Hochschule der Künste in Berlin and at the Central School of Art & Design in London. She lives and works in Berlin.

Dieter Appelt was born in Niemegk, Germany, in 1935. He lives and works in Berlin, where he has been a professor at the Hochschule der Künste since 1982.

Ingeborg Bachmann was born in Klagenfurt, Austria, in 1926. She studied philosophy in Vienna, and concluded her studies in 1950 with a dissertation on Martin Heidegger. In 1953, she became a member of the *Gruppe 47*, a society of German-language writers, formed after World War II. She wrote poetry, radio plays, short stories, and novels. She died in Rome in 1973.

Iain Bamforth currently runs his own medical practice in Strasbourg, France. He contributes frequently to the *Times Literary Supplement* and other journals, and is at work on a collection of essays.

Max Beckmann was born in Leipzig, Germany, in 1884. He studied at the Kunstschule in Weimar from 1900 to 1903, and lived in Paris and Florence before moving to Berlin in 1906. The first retrospective of his work was mounted in 1913, shortly before he enlisted as a voluntary medical officer in World War I. He was discharged in 1915 after suffering a mental breakdown, an experience that greatly affected his work. His influences during this period included Gnostic spiritual teachings, Buddhism, the Kabbala, and Schopenhauer. In 1937, the Nazis exhibited his work in the *Entartete Kunst (Degenerate Art)* show. He lived in exile in Amsterdam for the following ten years, and in 1947 moved to the United States to teach at Washington University's School of Art. He then taught at the Brooklyn Museum Art School in New York, until his death in 1950.

Wolf Biermann, a poet, songwriter and folksinger, was born in Hamburg in 1936. He settled in East Berlin after the Second World War. In 1965, the East German government banned some of his works, and he became a symbolic figure for fellow artists and dissidents. In 1976, while traveling in West Germany, Biermann spoke critically of the German Democratic Republic, prompting the East German government to strip him of his citizenship. The German National

Foundation awarded Biermann the second National Prize in 1998, in recognition of his contributions to Germany's cultural reunification, both before and after the country was reunited.

Karl Blossfeldt was born in Schielo, Germany, in 1865. He studied at the Royal Arts and Crafts Museum in Berlin, and then traveled throughout Italy, Greece, and North Africa collecting plant specimens. He returned to Berlin in 1896, and in 1898 became a professor at the College of Arts and Crafts there. He photographed plants for his work as a sculptor and art teacher; the pictures were originally his models, but they came to be appreciated in their own right. In 1928, Blossfeldt published a collection of photographs, *Elementary Forms of Art*. His prints were admired for their sharp focus and direct lighting, a departure from the soft-focus techniques of the period. He published a second book of photography just before his death in 1932.

John Bock was born in Gribbohm, Germany, in 1965. He studied at the Hochschule für Bildende Künste in Hamburg. He lives and works in Berlin.

Monica Bonvicini was born in 1965. She lives and works in Berlin and Los Angeles.

Volker Braun was born in Dresden, Germany, in 1939 and trained as a printer and machinist. He then studied philosophy in Leipzig and went on to become dramaturge at the Berliner Ensemble and the Deutsche Theater from 1965 to 1988. His honors include the Heinrich Mann Prize (1980), the East German National Prize (1988), and the Schiller Memorial Prize (1992). His collections of poetry include *Training des aufrechten Ganges* (1979) and *Langsam knirschender Morgen* (1987). The poems included here appeared in his most recent collection, *Tumulus*, published by Suhrkamp Verlag in 1999.

Bertolt Brecht was born in Augsburg, Bavaria, in 1898. He started writing plays and poetry during the First World War. His career in leftist, avant-garde theater was interrupted in 1933, when he had to leave Berlin and go into exile—first in Denmark and then, fleeing the advancing German army, in Sweden, Finland, and the United States. He lived in California from 1941 to 1947 and returned to East Berlin in 1949, where he cofounded the Berliner Ensemble with Helene Weigel. He died in 1956

John Burgan was born in London in 1962 and studied literature at the University of Newcastle upon Tyne. After working as picture editor for the BBC in London, Burgan attended the National Film & Television School. Since 1992, he has been living and working in Berlin as a writer and director. *Memory of Berlin* is the first full-length film he has directed.

Peter Constantine has written widely on the languages and cultures of East Asia. His work has been published in *Grand Street*, *The New Yorker*, and *Harper's Magazine*, among other publications. He was awarded the 1998 PEN/Book-of-the-Month Club Translation Prize for *Six Early Stories* by Thomas Mann (Sun & Moon Press). With Bradford Morrow he co-edited the "Radical Shadows" issue of *Conjunctions*. His most recent book of translations is *The Undiscovered Chekhov: Thirty-Eight New Stories* (Seven Stories Press).

Stig Dagerman was born in Alvkarleby, Sweden, in 1923. By the age of twenty-six, Dagerman had published four novels, a collection of short stories, a book of travel sketches, and four full-length plays.

His prolific career was cut short by his untimely death in 1954.

László Darvasi was born in Tÿrÿkszentmiklós, Hungary, in 1962. He has published poetry and seven volumes of stories, and has received many grants and awards. His work has been translated into German, French, and Dutch. His first novel, *A kÿnnymutatv´nyosok legend´ja*, was published in May 1999. He lives in Szeged, in southern Hungary.

Mike Davis is a contributing editor to *Grand Street*. He is currently completing a book titled *Late Victorian Holocausts: El Niño Famines and the Making of the Third World* (Verso, February 2000).

Margot Bettauer Dembo is a translator and editor. She won the Goethe-Institut/Berlin Translator's Prize in 1994–1995. Her recent translations include *Aftertime*, a novel by Olaf Georg Klein; *The Triumph of Hope*, by Ruth Elias; and *Europa, Europa*, by Solomon Perel.

Otto Dix was born in Gera, Germany, in 1891. He studied at the Kunstgewerbeschule in Dresden from 1909 until 1914, when he enlisted in the army. A collection of his war drawings was exhibited in Dresden in 1916. He developed a painting style using a sixteenth-century glazing technique, which lent a tone of realism to his depictions of modern warfare and corruption. He moved to Berlin in 1924, but returned to Dresden three years later to teach at the Kunstakademie. Although he was dismissed from his post in 1933 and labeled a "degenerate artist" by the Nazis, Dix continued to live in Germany and to exhibit his work abroad. In 1939, he was accused of conspiring to assassinate Hitler, and in 1945 he was drafted into the German army.

After the war he remained in Germany until his death in 1969.

Duncan Dobbelmann's translations of Louis Couperus and Paul van Ostaijen have appeared in *Conjunctions* and on the literary website *The Transcendental Friend*. He is currently writing his dissertation on the poet George Oppen.

Dogfilm is a video collective that was founded in Berlin, in 1991. Its five members, Bettina Ellerkamp, Jörg Heitmann, Merle Kröger, Ed van Megen, and Philip Scheffner produce video works from conception to post-production, many of them for German television stations such as ZDF, Kanal 4, and ARTE. In 1999, Dogfilm's television play *killer.berlin.doc* had its world premiere at the Internationales Forum des jungen Films in Berlin. The group is currently working on a documentary for ARTE, titled *Kein Mensch ist Illegal (No Human Is Illegal)*.

Maria Eichhorn was born in 1962. She currently lives in Berlin.

Daniel Eisenberg's films have been shown at the Museum of Modern Art, New York, the Centre Georges Pompidou, Paris, and the Kino Arsenal in Berlin. He has received many awards and fellowships, including a John Simon Guggenheim Memorial Foundation fellowship for 1999, the DAAD Berliner Künstlerprogramm Fellowship, 1991–1992 and 1997, and a National Endowment for the Arts Media Fellowship. He currently lives in Chicago and teaches in the Film Department at the School of the Art Institute of Chicago.

Harald Fricke was born in 1963. He has been the art and architecture editor of *die tageszeitung* since 1993, and a correspondent for *Artforum* since 1994. He lives in Berlin.

Robin Fulton was born in Scotland, in 1917. He has published several volumes of poetry, including *Selected Poems 1963–1978* (Macdonald, Edinburgh, 1980), and *Fields of Focus* (Anvil Press, London, 1982). He has also translated the work of several Swedish writers, including Stig Dagerman, Pär Lagerkvist, and Tomas Tranströmer. Fulton received the Artur Lundkvist award for Swedish translation in 1977, and the Swedish Academy award in 1978.

(e.) Twin Gabriel is an art collaborative. Its members, Else Gabriel and Ullf Wrede, have been working together since 1990. They live in Berlin.

Gerrit Gohlke is an art critic and freelance writer. He was born in 1968, and has lived in Berlin since 1989. He has been the co-editor of *Be Magazin* since 1994, and is head of the Media Arts Lab in Berlin.

Erdağ M. Göknar is a writer and translator and lives between Seattle and Istanbul. He has an M.F.A. in creative writing and is completing a Ph.D. in Ottoman and Turkish Studies at the University of Washington. He is currently translating *My Name Is Crimson*, the most recent novel by Orhan Pamuk.

Günter Grass was born in Danzig (now Gdansk, Poland), in 1927. He fought in World War II and spent 1945 and 1946 as a prisoner of war in Czechoslovakia. During his twenties, he studied stonemasonry and sculpture, and attended both the Academy of Art in Düsseldorf and the State Academy of Fine Arts in Berlin. He has been a farm laborer, apprentice stonecutter, miner and jazz musician. He has written plays, poetry and essays, and was a speechwriter for Willy Brandt during his tenure as mayor of West Berlin. Grass is best known for his novel *The Tin Drum*, which was published in 1959 and later made into a film. He has received numerous literary awards and holds honorary doctorates from Kenyon College and Harvard University. He lives in Berlin.

Matthew Griffin teaches in the Department of Comparative Literature at Hofstra University.

George Grosz was born Georg Ehrenfried Gross in 1893. From 1909 to 1912 he attended the Academy of Arts in Dresden. In 1915, after a short stint in the army, he returned to Berlin and changed his name to George Grosz to protest anti-English propaganda. His first portfolio of prints was published in 1917, and between 1919 and 1933 he contributed to many satirical journals in Weimar Germany. He moved to New York in 1933 to teach at the Art Students League and became an American citizen. His eventual disenchantment with the United States prompted him to move back to Berlin, where he died shortly after his return in 1959.

Durs Grünbein was born in 1962 in Dresden, Germany, and has lived in Berlin since 1985. He is the recipient of many prizes, including the 1995 Georg Büchner Prize, and is the author of five collections of poetry, most recently *Nach den Satiren* (1999), and a collection of essays, *Galilei vermißt Dantes Hölle und bleibt an den Maßen hängen* (1996).

Hans Haacke was born in Cologne, Germany, in 1936. He studied at the Hochschule für Bildende Künste in Kassel from 1956 to 1960. He currently lives and works in New York.

Doug Hall received his M.F.A. in sculpture from The Maryland Institute College of Art. His work has been exhibited in many museums in the United States and Europe, including the San Francisco Museum of

Modern Art, the Museum of Modern Art, New York, and the Berlinische Galerie, Berlin. He is a professor at the San Francisco Art Institute, where he has taught in the New Genres Department since 1981.

John Hamilton was born in New York, in 1963. After a decade of recording and touring with his band Tiny Lights, he studied at New York University, where he received his Ph.D. in Comparative Literature. He is currently a visiting professor of Classics at the University of California, Santa Cruz.

Mark Harman has taught German and Irish literature at Dartmouth, Oberlin College, and the University of Pennsylvania. His translations include *Robert Walser Rediscovered: Stories, Fairy-Tale Plays, and Critical Responses* (Dartmouth College/University Press of New England), and *The Castle* by Franz Kafka (Schocken Books).

Marsden Hartley was born in 1877. He had his first one-man exhibition in 1909 at Alfred Stieglitz's "291" Gallery in New York. In 1912, he traveled to Paris and Berlin, where his work was included in the Blaue Reiter exhibit. After his return to the United States, he took part in the Armory Show, experimented with Constructivist techniques, and finally made a transition toward Primitivism. He died in 1943.

Raoul Hausmann was born in Vienna in 1886 and moved to Berlin with his family in 1900. As a young man, he created expressionist lithographs and woodcuts, and published art criticism in several Berlin magazines. In 1919, he and Johannes Baader founded the journal *Der Dada*, and a collection of Hausmann's photomontages was exhibited at the First International Dada Fair in 1920. Hausmann left Germany for Ibiza in 1933, but fled to France in 1936 to avoid the Spanish Fascists. He lived in France for the rest of his life, where he painted and experimented with photography and sound poetry. He died in 1971.

John Heartfield was born Helmut Herzfeld in 1891, in Berlin. An aversion to military service and an interest in drawing led Heartfield to the writer/painter George Grosz, with whom he developed the photomontage technique. From 1930 to 1938 he contributed to the periodical *Arbeiter Illustrierte Zeitung*, producing full-page admonitions against Hitler and the threat of war. Heartfield's inventive use of photomontage influenced much of the political art of the 1960s. He died in Berlin in 1968.

Michael Henry Heim teaches Russian and Central European Literature at the University of California, Los Angeles. He translates from the Russian, Czech, Serbo-Croatian, Hungarian, German, and French. His translations include works by Anton Chekhov and Milan Kundera, as well as a biography of Chekhov written by Henri Troyat.

Judith Hermann was born in 1970 in Berlin, where she lives and works as a writer and journalist. The story published here appeared in her first collection of short stories, *Sommerhaus, später* (S. Fischer Verlag, 1998).

Hannah Höch was born in Thüringen, Germany, in 1889. An avant-garde artist known for her ties to the Berlin Dada group, she was one of the originators of photomontage. Her best-known works are approximately eighty photomontages she produced between 1918 and 1933, that commented on the "New

German Woman" and the rise of Facism. She died in Berlin in 1978.

Michael Hofmann is a poet and translator of German prose, including works by Bertolt Brecht, Franz Kafka, and Joseph Roth. He has received the Cholmondeley Award, the Geoffrey Faber Memorial Prize and the International IMPAC Dublin Literary Award. Hoffman is the author of *After Ovid: New Metamorphoses* (Noonday Press) and *K.S. in Lakeland: New and Selected Poems* (Ecco Press).

Felicitas Hoppe was born in Hameln, Germany, in 1960. She studied literature and rhetoric in Tübingen, Berlin, Rome, and the United States. Her collection of stories, *Picknick der Friseure*, was published in Germany by Rowohlt in 1996; her novel *Pigafetta* was published by Rowohlt in 1999. She currently lives in Berlin.

Sabine Hornig was born in Pforzheim, Germany, in 1964. She studied at the Hochschule der Künste in Berlin from 1986 to 1992. She currently lives in Berlin.

Jörg Immendorff was born in Bleckede, Germany, in 1945. He studied art under Joseph Beuys at the Kunstakademie in Düsseldorf, where he currently lives and works.

Lotte Jacobi was born into a family of portrait photographers. She spent the 1920s and 1930s documenting Berlin's avant-garde, in photographs of figures such as Kurt Weill, Peter Lorre, and Lotte Lenya, among others, before moving to New York in 1935. Her many American portrait subjects include Eleanor Roosevelt and J.D. Salinger. She now lives in Derry, New Hampshire.

Johannes Kahrs was born in Bremen, Germany, in 1965. From 1988 to 1994 he studied at the Hochschule der Künste in Berlin. He lives and works in Berlin.

Edward and **Nancy Reddin Kienholz** began collaborating in 1972. The first full-scale survey of their work was exhibited at the Whitney Museum of American Art, New York, in 1996, the Museum of Contemporary Art, Los Angeles, and the Berlinische Galerie, Berlin. Edward Kienholz died in Hope, Idaho, in 1994. Nancy Reddin Kienholz continues to live and work in Hope.

Martin Kippenberger was born in Dortmund, Germany, in 1953. He died in Vienna in 1997.

Sarah Kirsch was born in 1935 in Limlingrode, Germany, and studied biology and literature in Leipzig. She moved to West Berlin in 1977 and has lived in Schleswig-Holstein since 1983. Her most recent poetry publications are *Erlkönigs Tochter* (1992) and *Ich, Crusoe* (1996). She has been awarded the Hölderlin, Huchel, and Büchner prizes.

Hermann Kleinknecht was born in 1950 in Bad Berneck/Oberfranken, Germany, and lives in Munich.

Andreas Koch was born in Stuttgart, Germany, in 1970.

Jane Kramer writes the "Letter from Europe" for *The New Yorker*. Her last book was *The Politics of Memory* (Random House, 1996) and her next will be about a militia community in northwestern Washington state. She lives in Paris and New York.

Günter Kunert was born in Berlin in 1929. His mother's family was deported to concentration camps when he was a child. Kunert studied graphic arts in Berlin, and in 1976 he moved to Itzehoe in northern Germany. He has received many prizes for his work, which has been published by Carl Hanser Verlag since 1963.

Maude Lavin is the author of *Cut with the Kitchen Knife: A Monograph on Hannah Höch*. She is now completing *Clean New World: Cultural Issues and Graphic Design from John Heartfield to the Internet*.

Karl-Hartmut Lerch was born in Bohlheim, Germany, in 1943. He lives in Paris and Berlin.

Via Lewandowsky was born in Dresden, Germany, in 1963. He studied at the Hochschule für Bildende Künste in Dresden from 1982 to 1987. He lives and works in Berlin and New York.

Jeanne Mammen was born in Berlin in 1890. She grew up in Paris and studied in Brussels and Rome before returning to Berlin in 1915. While living in Paris, she drew illustrations for works by Gustave Flaubert and E.T.A. Hoffmann. In Berlin during the 1920s and 1930s, she made her living as a fashion and general illustrator, contributing her work to magazines, advertising brochures, joke books and satirical journals. Her first exhibition was mounted in 1930, but in 1932 the Nazis banned a collection of her lithographs. She remained in Berlin throughout the war, working as a firefighter, and began to exhibit her work again in 1947. She died in Berlin in 1976.

Arwed Messmer was born in Schopfheim, Germany, in 1964. He studied visual communications and photo design at the Fachhochschule Dortmund, and received the National Award from Kodak Germany in 1991 and the Otto Steinart Prize from the German Society for Photography in 1995. His work has been included in the permanent collection of the Berlinische Galerie. He lives in Berlin.

John Miller was born in Cleveland, Ohio, in 1954. He lives in New York and Berlin.

Heiner Müller was born in Eppendorf, Germany, in 1929. In the early 1950s, he was employed by the East German Writers' Union, but when his play *The Resettler* was closed by German Democratic Republic authorities after dress rehearsals in 1961, he was expelled from the Union. In 1959, along with his wife and collaborator Inge Müller, he was awarded the Heinrich Mann Prize. He was also awarded the Georg Büchner Prize in 1985 and the Kleist Prize in 1990. In 1991, he became part of the new group leadership of the Berliner Ensemble, and in 1995 its sole artistic director. He died in 1995.

Inge Müller was born Ingeborg Meyer in Berlin in 1925. She worked as a freelance writer beginning in 1953, publishing journalism and children's books as well as poetry and prose. She met Heiner Müller the same year and married him in 1955. They collaborated often over the next few years, and in 1959 shared the Heinrich Mann Prize. In 1966, Inge Müller committed suicide in Berlin.

Joachim Neugroschel has translated over 175 books from the French, German, Italian, Russian, and Yiddish. He has won three PEN Translation Prizes as well as the French-American Translation Prize, and is a Chevalier in France's Order of Arts and Letters. He is currently working on several Yiddish anthologies.

Cees Nooteboom is the author of *In the Dutch Mountains, Rituals, The Following Story*, and many other books of fiction, poetry, travel literature, and nonfiction. In 1993, he was awarded the European Literary Prize for best novel, and in 1982 his novel *Rituals* was awarded the Pegasus Prize for Literature.

Felix Nussbaum was born in Osnabrück, Germany, in 1904. He attended the Staatliche Kunstgewerbeschule in Hamburg, and moved to Berlin in 1923 to study art at the Vereinigte Staatsschulen für freie und angewandte Kunst. He left Germany for Belgium in 1933, after the Nazis withdrew an art scholarship he had been awarded. Although he was forbidden to work, Nussbaum continued to participate in exhibitions in Holland and France. In 1940, he spent several months in an internment camp in southern France, and in 1942 he went into hiding. He was captured in 1944 and sent to Auschwitz, where he was killed the same year.

Brigitte Oleschinski was born in 1955 in Cologne, Germany, and lives in Berlin. She studied political science and worked until recently as a modern historian with a special interest in the German resistance to Hitler. She is now a full-time writer, and has published two volumes of poetry. The poems that appear in this issue were taken from her most recent volume, *Your Passport Is Not Guilty* (1997, Rowohlt Verlag).

Aras Ören was born in Istanbul in 1939. He is an award-winning writer who worked as an actor and dramaturge before moving to Berlin in 1969. His poems, stories and novels, often dealing with issues of race, discrimination, and exile, have appeared in German and Turkish editions.

Olivier Ortolani was born in 1955 and studied theater and literature in Berlin and Paris. He has published books in Germany on Dario Fo and Peter Brook, and has written articles and interviews for German, French, and Belgian magazines.

Albert Ostermaier was born in Munich in 1967. In 1990, he received Munich's Literature Stipend, and in 1995 he was awarded the PEN/Liechtenstein Prize for Lyric Poetry. He was the 1996/1997 writer-in-residence at the National Theater in Mannheim. In 1997, he was commissioned by the Bavarian *Staatsschauspiel* to write a piece celebrating the one hundredth anniversary of Bertolt Brecht's birth. Ostermaier is the fourth recipient of the Hubert von Herkorner Prize. *Tartar Titus* won the Translator Prize from the Goethe Institute in 1998.

Emine Sevgi Özdamar was born in Malatya, Turkey, in 1946. Her first collection of short stories, *Mutterzunge* (Rotbuch Verlag) was published in 1990. She is also the author of the novels *Das Leben ist eine Karawanserei hat zwei Türen aus einer kam ich rein aus der anderen ging ich raus* and *Die Brücke vom Goldenen Horn* (both published by Kiepenheuer & Witsch), from which "The Long Corridors of the Women's Dormitory" is excerpted.

Oskar Pastior was born in 1927 in Hermannstadt, Romania. In 1944 he was deported to a work camp in Ukraine, where he remained until 1949. Upon his release, he returned to his hometown and worked at a sporting goods factory. From 1955 to 1960 he studied German philology in Bucharest, and settled eventually in Berlin. Among several other awards, he has received the Ernst Meister Prize (1986) and Hugo Ball Prize (1990), and held the Poetics Lectureship in Frankfurt for 1993–1994. His most recent books are

Knopfnuß Januskopf (1990); *Vokalismen&Gimpelstifte* (1992); *Eine kleine Kunstmaschine: 34 Sestinen* (1994); and *Das Hören des Genitivs* (1998).

A.R. Penck was born in 1939 in Dresden, Germany. Since 1989 he has been teaching at the Kunstakademie in Düsseldorf.

Manfred Pernice was born in Hildesheim in 1963. From 1984 to 1987 he studied at the Hochschule für Bildende Künste in Braunschweig, and from 1988 to 1993 at the Hochschule der Künste in Berlin. He currently lives and works in Berlin.

Burton Pike's translations have appeared in *Conjunctions, Fiction,* and *Dimension,* among other publications. He edited and co-translated *Precision and Soul* (University of Chicago Press), the selected essays of Robert Musil, and Musil's novel *The Man Without Qualities* (Knopf).

Cay-Sophie Rabinowitz is U.S. Senior Editor of *Parkett* magazine. She studied comparative literature with Jean-François Lyotard at Emory University in Atlanta. A writer and critic, she is contributing editor for *Art Papers* and has published widely on contemporary art.

Christian Rattemeyer is a graduate student in the Ph.D. program in the Department of Art History at Columbia University. He was the founder and co-director of the independent project space *Osmos* in Berlin, and in 1999 he received an M.A. in Art History from the Freie Universität in Berlin. He is a regular contributor to *Blitz Review*, an art magazine on the Internet. He lives in New York.

Neo Rauch was born in Leipzig in 1960. He studied at the Hochschule für Grafik und Buchkunst from 1981 to 1986.

Raffael Rheinsberg was born in Kiel, Germany, in 1943. From 1973 to 1979 he studied at the Fachhochschule für Gestaltung in Kiel. He currently lives and works in Berlin.

Rivka Rinn was born in Tel Aviv in 1950, and now lives in Berlin.

Aura Rosenberg was born in New York City. She lives in New York and Berlin.

Joseph Roth was born Moses Joseph Roth in 1894. His family belonged to the large Orthodox Jewish community in Brody, then part of the Austro-Hungarian Empire. He studied literature at the University of Lemberg (Lvov) from 1914 to 1916, and served in the Austrian Army from 1916 to 1918. He wrote for Austrian and German newspapers, published poetry, short stories, essays and serialized novels, and traveled throughout Eastern Europe during the 1920s. Roth's writings explored his two great interests: the experience of East European Jews in postwar Western Europe, and the decline of the Austro-Hungarian Empire. He moved to Paris when Hitler became Chancellor of Germany, and died in exile there in 1939.

Sabine Russ is a German art critic and curator based in New York. She has contributed to numerous exhibition catalogues in Europe and in the United States. She is the coauthor (with Jens Henkel) of a bibliographical book on self-published artists' books and journals in the former German Democratic Republic, *D1980D1989R, Künstlerbücher und originalgrafische Zeitschriften im Eigenverlag.*

Ivan Sanders is Professor of English at Suffolk County Community College and Adjunct Professor at Columbia University. He has translated works by Milán Füst, George Konrád, and Péter Nádas. His translation of George Konrád's novel *Stone Dial* will be published by Harcourt Brace in the spring of 2000.

Joachim Sartorius was born in 1946 and lives in Munich, where he is the General Secretary of the Goethe Institute. He is the author of three volumes of poetry, most recently *Keiner gefriert anders*, and the translator of John Ashbery, William Carlos Williams, and Wallace Stevens.

Christian Schad was born in Miesbach, Bavaria, in 1894. He studied painting at the Munich Academy of Art, and in 1915 he exhibited in the Munich Secession. The same year, he moved to Switzerland to avoid fighting in the army. He lived in Zürich and Geneva, working as a graphic artist and experimenting with photographic techniques. In 1919, he and the writer Walter Serner founded Geneva Dada and organized the first Dadaist "World Congress" in Geneva. Schad moved to Berlin in 1927 and spent several years there painting. He left Berlin in 1942 and died in Keilberg in 1982.

Frieder Schnock was born in Meissen, Germany, in 1953. He currently lives and works in Berlin.

Ingo Schulze was born in Dresden, Germany, in 1962 and studied classical philology at the University of Jena. His first book, *33 Moments of Happiness*, won both the Döblin Prize and the Sillner Prize for Literature. The two stories published here are from his forthcoming collection, *Simple Stories*, to be published by Knopf in the spring of 2000. He lives in Berlin.

Andrew Shields received a Ph.D. in Comparative Literature from the University of Pennsylvania in 1995. He lives in Basel, Switzerland, where he teaches English at the University of Basel. His poetry, prose, and translations have appeared in *Poetry*, *PN Review*, *International Quarterly*, and *Mr. Knife, Miss Fork*.

Kristina Solomoukha was born in Kiev, Ukraine, in 1971. She lives and works in Berlin and Paris.

Heidi Specker was born in Damme, Germany, in 1962 and currently lives in Berlin.

Erik Steinbrecher was born in Basel, Switzerland, in 1963. He lives in Zürich and Berlin.

Renata Stih was born in Zagreb, Croatia, in 1955. She currently lives and works in Berlin.

Lois Weinberger was born in Stams, Austria, in 1947. He lives in Vienna.

Peter Weiss was born near Berlin in 1916. In 1934, his family emigrated to England. After living in England and Switzerland, he studied at the Academy of Art in Prague and then took Swedish citizenship. Weiss became a painter, newspaper correspondent, film director and novelist before finding his calling in the theater. His 1964 play, *The Persecution and Assassination of Jean-Paul Marat as Performed by the Inmates of the Asylum of Charenton under the Direction of the Marquis de Sade*, which was later made into a film directed by Peter Brook, won Weiss international acclaim. He died in 1982.

Olav Westphalen was born in Hamburg in 1963. From 1984 to 1988 he studied at the Fachhochschule für Gestaltung in Hamburg, and from 1990 to 1993 he was an M.F.A. student at the University of California, San Diego. He lives in New York and Berlin.

John E. Woods's translations include Arno Schmidt's *Evening Edged in Gold*, for which he won the American Book Award for translation; Patrick Süskind's *Perfume*; Ingo Schulze's *33 Moments of Happiness*; and several novels by Thomas Mann. For his translations of *The Magic Mountain* and Arno Schmidt's *Nobodaddy's Children*, he was presented the first Helen and Kurt Wolff Prize for Translation from the German in 1996.

Peter Zadek was born in Berlin in 1926 and emigrated to England in 1933. He attended Oxford University and studied theater direction at the Old Vic School in London, where he staged his first productions before returning to Germany in the late 1950s. In 1992, he joined the group directorship of the Berliner Ensemble, the theater originally founded by Bertolt Brecht and Helene Weigel. He left the group in 1995.

Grand Street would like to thank the following people for their generous support:

Edward Lee Cave
Cathy and Stephen Graham
Betty and Stanley Sheinbaum

★ ★ ★

We also thank:

Benjamin Anastas
Perry Anderson
Kathrin Becker
Olivier Berggruen
Sebastian Brecht
Ingke Brodersen
Peter Constantine
Lo Dagerman
Carol Eckman
Erdağ M.Göknar
Carol Greene
John Hamilton
Petra Hardt
Andrea Heyde
William Horrigan
Radhika Jones
Michael Kazmarek
Jane Kramer
Friedrich Loock
Chris Marker

Alberta Mayo
Jackie McAllister
Christopher Middleton
John Miller
David Nolan
Meghan O'Rourke
Klaus Pohl
Cay-Sophie Rabinowitz
Christian Rattemeyer
Barbara Richter
Aura Rosenberg
Gereon Sievernich
Fritz Stern
Christoph Tannert
Daniel Theisen
Frank Wagner
Sanda Weigel
Olav Westphalen
Drenka Willen
Hanns Zischler

ILLUSTRATIONS

Front Cover
Hannah Höch, *Das Fest kann beginnen (On with the Party)*, 1965. Photomontage, 10 7/16 x 13 3/4 in. Collection Institut für Auslandsbeziehungen, Stuttgart. Copyright © Artists Rights Society (ARS), New York/VG Bild-Kunst, Bonn.

Back Cover
Arwed Messmer, *City #04*, 1995. C-print. Courtesy of the artist.

Title Page
Doug Hall, *Congress Hall of the United Socialist Party of Germany (SED), Central Committee Building, Berlin*, from the series *The GDR Project*, 1992. Black-and-white photograph, 61 x 48 in. Courtesy of the artist, Kapinos, Berlin, and Feigen Contemporary, New York.

Table of Contents
East Berlin border guards on top of the Berlin Wall, 1989. Photo credit: Corbis/Reuters.

pp. 25–28 Four photomontages by Hannah Höch. Titles and dates appear with images. **p. 25** 10 7/16 x 13 3/4 in. Collection Institut für Auslandsbeziehungen, Stuttgart. **p. 26** 12 13/16 x 5 7/8 in. Collection Institut für Auslandsbeziehungen, Stuttgart. **p. 27** 13 1/2 x 16 in. Collection Landesbank, Berlin. **p. 28** 14 15/16 x 12 5/8 in. Collection Berlinische Galerie, Landesmuseum für Moderne Kunst, Photographie und Architektur, Berlin. All images copyright © Artists Rights Society (ARS), New York/VG Bild-Kunst, Bonn.

p. 33 Great Altar of Pergamon. Photo credit: Corbis/Ruggero Vanni

pp. 54–65 A portfolio of eleven artworks. Artists, titles, and dates appear with images. **p. 54** Black-and-white photograph. Courtesy of the Lotte Jacobi Archives, Photographic Services and Special Collections, University of New Hampshire, Durham, New Hampshire. **p. 55** Lithograph on imitation Japan paper, image: 17 5/8 x 12 5/8 in., paper: 23 x 17 13/16 in. Collection Sprengel Museum, Hannover. **pp. 56–57** Oil on wood, three panels: **(left)** 71 1/4 x 39 3/4 in., **(center)** 71 1/4 x 79 1/8 in., **(right)** 71 1/4 x 39 3/8 in. Collection Galerie der Stadt, Stuttgart. **p. 58** Lithograph on paper, 11 3/8 x 8 5/8 in. Collection Berlinische Galerie, Landesmuseum für Moderne Kunst, Photographie und Architektur, Berlin. **p. 59** From *AIZ* Vol. II, No. 34, August 21, 1932. Offset version of photomontage on paper, 14 1/4 x 10 5/8 in. Akron Art Museum, Ohio, Museum Acquisition Fund. **p. 60** Watercolor and pencil on paper, 17 3/4 x 14 in. Des Moines Art Center Permanent Collections, gift of Dr. Joseph H. Seipp, Baltimore, Maryland. Photo credit: Ray Andrews. **p. 61** Oil on canvas, 35 7/16 x 23 5/8 in. Collection Staatliche Museen zu Berlin, Preussischer Kulturbesitz Nationalgalerie, Berlin. Photo credit: Jörg P. Anders, Berlin. **p. 62** Collage and gouache on cardboard, 12 3/16 x 14 9/16 in. Collection Galerie Berinson, Berlin. **p. 63** Oil on canvas, 39 3/8 x 32 5/16 in. Niedersächsischen Sparkassenstiftung Felix Nussbaum Collection, Kulturgeschichtliches Museum, Osnabrück. **p. 64** Oil on canvas, 32 1/4 x 21 1/2 in. Collection Frederick R. Weisman Art Museum at the University of Minnesota, images copyright © Artists Rights Society (ARS), New York/VG Bild-Kunst, Bonn except **pp. 58, 62, 63, 64, and 65. p. 62** Copyright © Artists Rights Society (ARS), New York/ADAGP, Paris. **p. 65** Copyright © Karl Blossfeldt Archiv, Ann und Jürgen Wilde, Cologne/Artists Rights Society (ARS), New York.

pp. 81–84 Portfolio of five photographs by four artists. Titles and dates appear with images. **p. 81** C-print. Courtesy of the artist. **p. 82 (left and right)** Both works inkjet on aluminum, 43 5/16 x 35 7/16 in. each. **p. 83** C-print, 61 x 48 in. Courtesy of the artist, Kapinos, Berlin, and Feigen Contemporary, New York. **p. 84** C-print, 8 x 10 in. Courtesy of the artist, Galerie Barbara Weiss, Berlin, and Metro Pictures, New York.

p. 92 Dugway Proving Ground, Utah. Photo credit: Ted Givens

pp. 103–108 Six pages (numbers 1, 9, 15, 19, 25, and 47) from Bertolt Brecht's *War Primer*. First published as *Kriegsfibel* by Eulenspiegel Verlag, Berlin, 1955; second edition 1994. Published by Libris, London, 1998. **p. 103** #25: Caption reads "British Bombers Over Berlin. In late summer 1940 the RAF mounted several raids in Hamburg, Bremen and other major German towns of industrial and military importance. The British bombed Berlin for the first time on 10/11 September. The picture shows a house in Berlin after a British raid." Poem dated December 24, 1940. Photo from an unidentified Swedish magazine of October, 1940. **p. 104** #19: Poem dated August 4, 1940. Photo reputedly from an unidentified Swedish paper of January 20, 1942. **p. 105** #9: Poem attributed to 1944. Cutting dated July 17, following the French armistice. Roubaix is on the frontier with Belgium. **p. 106** #15: Poem dated May 20, 1940. Photo of Winston Churchill from an unidentified Swedish magazine of June, 1940. **p. 107** #1: Adolf Hitler. Poem dated March 14, 1940. **p. 108** #47: Poem attributed to 1944. Photo from *Life*, January 19, 1942, shows the film actress Jane Wyman in an RAF blue dress. *Life* copyright © Time, Inc.

pp. 133–137 Portfolio of five works by four artists. Titles and dates appear with images. **p. 133** Mixed media, dimensions variable. Courtesy of the artist and Mehdi Chouakri, Berlin. **p. 134** Site specific installation, transparency mounted on glass and fabricated wall. Photo credit: Peter Pachano. Courtesy of the artist. **p. 135** Mural, 213 x 259 13/16 x 7 7/8 in. Courtesy of the artist and Galerie Barbara Weiss, Berlin. **p. 136** Glass sheet, 98 7/16 x 59 in. Courtesy of the artist and Mehdi Chouakri, Berlin. **p. 137** Fabricated door and balcony. Courtesy of the artist and Galerie Barbara Weiss, Berlin.

pp. 152–156 Portfolio of five works by five artists.. Titles and dates appear with images. **p. 152** Black-and-white laser print, 11 x 8 1/2 in. Courtesy of the artists and Galerie Barbara Thumm, Berlin. **p. 153** Mixed media, 78 3/4 x 98 7/16 x 70 7/8 in. Courtesy of the artist, Galerie Neu, Berlin, and Anton Kern Gallery, New York. **p. 154** Cardboard, 14 1/2 x 19 3/4 x 10 1/4 in. Courtesy of the artist and Michael Werner Gallery, New York and Cologne **p. 155 (left)** Silkscreen print mounted on shipboard, 15 3/4 x 19 11/16 x 19 11/16 in. (one module). **(right)** Fory-eight modules, 189 x 47 1/4 x 47 1/4 in. Courtesy of the artist. **p. 156** Painting on fiberboard on wood, variable dimensions. Courtesy of the artist and Zwinger Galerie, Berlin.

GRAND STREET
BACK ISSUES

GRAND STREET 59 TIME

Fetishes

Egos

Dreams

Edward Ruscha
Luis Buñuel
Terry Southern
ADOBE LK
William

George

Dirt

GRAND STREET 58 DISGUISES

Marcel
Anjelic

GRAND STREET 60 PARANOIA

GRAND STREET 61 ALL-AMERICAN

ALL-AMERICAN 61
William T. Vollmann
Octavio Paz
Peter Sellars
Reinaldo Arenas
Mike Davis
Doris Salcedo

53   55   56   57

ORDER
WHILE THEY LAST

7 1/2 Ton Cube, 1990. Solid steel cube, white automotive lacquer. 36 × 36 × 36 in. Yes, 1990. Canvas framed portrait on canvas wall. dimensions variable. Fall '91. 1991. Enlarged fabricated mannequin, clothing, Puzzle Bottle, 1992. Glass bottle, assembled wood figure. paint. 13 × 3 × 4 × in.

CALL

212 533 2944

Please send name, address, issue number(s), and quantity.

American Express, Mastercard, and Visa accepted; please send credit-card number and expiration date. Back issues are $15 each ($18 overseas and Canada), including postage and handling, payable in U.S. dollars. Address orders to GRAND STREET, *Back Issues, 214 Sullivan Street no. 6c New York, NY 10012.*

Some of the bookstores where you can find

GRAND STREET

Magpie Magazine Gallery, Vancouver, CANADA

Newsstand, Bellingham, WA
Bailey Coy Books, Seattle, WA
Hideki Ohmori, Seattle, WA

Looking Glass Bookstore, Portland, OR
Powell's Books, Portland, OR
Reading Frenzy, Portland, OR

...On Sundays, Tokyo, JAPAN

ASUC Bookstore, Berkeley, CA
Black Oak Books, Berkeley, CA
Cody's Books, Berkeley, CA
Bookstore Fiona, Carson, CA
Huntley Bookstore, Claremont, CA
Book Soup, Hollywood, CA
University Bookstore, Irvine, CA
Museum of Contemporary Art, La Jolla, CA
UCSD Bookstore, La Jolla, CA
A.R.T. Press, Los Angeles, CA
Museum of Contemporary Art, Los Angeles, CA
Occidental College Bookstore, Los Angeles, CA
Sun & Moon Press Bookstore, Los Angeles, CA
UCLA/Armand Hammer Museum, Los Angeles, CA
Stanford Bookstore, Newark, CA
Diesel, A Bookstore, Oakland, CA
Blue Door Bookstore, San Diego, CA
Museum of Contemporary Art, San Diego, CA
The Booksmith, San Francisco, CA
City Lights, San Francisco, CA
Green Apple Books, San Francisco, CA
Modern Times Bookstore, San Francisco, CA
MuseumBooks–SF MOMA, San Francisco, CA
San Francisco Camerawork, San Francisco, CA
Logos, Santa Cruz, CA
Arcana, Santa Monica, CA
Midnight Special Bookstore, Santa Monica, CA
Reader's Books, Sonoma, CA
Small World Books, Venice, CA
Ventura Bookstore, Ventura, CA

Honolulu Book Shop, Honolulu, HI

Page One, SINGAPORE

Baxter's Books, Minneapolis, MN
Minnesota Book Center, Minneapolis, MN
University of Minnesota Bookstore, Minneapolis, MN
Walker Art Center Bookshop, Minneapolis, MN
Hungry Mind Bookstore, St. Paul, MN
Odegard Books, St. Paul, MN

Chinook Bookshop, Colorado Springs, CO
The Bookies, Denver, CO
Newsstand Cafe, Denver, CO
Tattered Cover Bookstore, Denver, CO
Stone Lion Bookstore, Fort Collins, CO

Nebraska Bookstore, Lincoln, NE

Asun Bookstore, Reno, NV

Sam Weller's Zion Bookstore, Salt Lake City, UT

Kansas Union Bookstore, Lawrence, KS
Terra Nova Bookstore, Lawrence, KS

Bookworks, Albuquerque, NM
Page One Bookstore, Albuquerque, NM
Salt of the Earth, Albuquerque, NM
Cafe Allegro, Los Alamos, NM
Collected Works, Santa Fe, NM

Bookman's, Tucson, AZ

Book People, Austin, TX
Bookstop, Austin, TX
University Co-op Society, Austin, TX
McKinney Avenue Contemporary Gift Shop, Dallas, TX
Bookstop, Houston, TX
Brazos Bookstore, Houston, TX
Contemporary Arts Museum Shop, Houston, TX
Diversebooks, Houston, TX
Menil Collection Bookstore, Houston, TX
Museum of Fine Arts, Houston, TX
Texas Gallery, Houston, TX
Bookstop, Plano, TX

Bookland of Brunswick, Brunswick, ME
University of Maine Bookstore, Orono, ME
Books Etc., Portland, ME
Raffles Cafe Bookstore, Portland, ME

Pages, Toronto, CANADA

Dartmouth Bookstore, Hanover, NH
Toadstool Bookshop, Peterborough, NH

Northshire Books, Manchester, VT

Wootton's Books, Amherst, MA
Boston University Bookstore, Boston, MA
Harvard Book Store, Cambridge, MA
M.I.T. Press Bookstore, Cambridge, MA
Cisco Harland Books, Marlborough, MA
Broadside Bookshop, Northampton, MA
Provincetown Bookshop, Provincetown, MA
Water Street Books, Williamstown, MA

Main Street News, Ann Arbor, MI
Shaman Drum Bookshop, Ann Arbor, MI
Cranbrook Art Museum Books, Bloomfield Hills, MI
Book Beat, Oak Park, MI

Accident or Design, Providence, RI
Brown University Bookstore, Providence, RI
College Hill Store, Providence, RI

Afterwords, Milwaukee, WI

Farley's Bookshop, New Hope, PA
Faber Books, Philadelphia, PA
Waterstone's Booksellers, Philadelphia, PA
Andy Warhol Museum, Pittsburgh, PA
Encore Books, Mechanicsburg, PA
Encore Books, State College, PA

Yale Cooperative, New Haven, CT
UConn Co-op, Storrs, CT

Rosetta News, Carbondale, IL
Pages for All Ages, Champaign, IL
Mayuba Bookstore, Chicago, IL
Museum of Contemporary Art, Chicago, IL
Seminary Co-op Bookstore, Chicago, IL

Indiana University Bookstore,
Bloomington, IN

UC Bookstore, Cincinnati, OH
Bank News, Cleveland, OH
Ohio State University Bookstore, Columbus, OH
Student Book Exchange, Columbus, OH
Books & Co., Dayton, OH
Kenyon College Bookstore, Gambier, OH
Oberlin Consumers Cooperative, Oberlin, OH

Encore Books, Princeton, NJ
Micawber Books, Princeton, NJ

Community Bookstore, Brooklyn, NY
Talking Leaves, Buffalo, NY
Colgate University Bookstore, Hamilton, NY
Book Revue, Huntington, NY
The Bookery, Ithaca, NY
A Different Light, New York, NY
Art Market, New York, NY
B. Dalton, New York, NY
Coliseum Books, New York, NY
Collegiate Booksellers, New York, NY
Doubleday Bookshops, New York, NY
Exit Art/First World Store, New York, NY
Gold Kiosk, New York, NY
Gotham Book Mart, New York, NY
Museum of Modern Art Bookstore, New York, NY
New York University Book Center, New York, NY
Posman Books, New York, NY
Rizzoli Bookstores, New York, NY
St. Mark's Bookshop, New York, NY
Shakespeare & Co., New York, NY
Spring Street Books, New York, NY
Wendell's Books, New York, NY
Whitney Museum of Modern Art, New York, NY
Syracuse University Bookstore, Syracuse, NY

Iowa Book & Supply, Iowa City, IA
Prairie Lights, Iowa City, IA
University Bookstore, Iowa City, IA

Box of Rocks, Bowling Green, KY
Carmichael's, Louisville, KY

Louie's Bookstore Cafe, Baltimore, MD

Xanadu Bookstore, Memphis, TN

Bridge Street Books, Washington, DC
Chapters, Washington, DC
Franz Bader Bookstore, Washington, DC
Olsson's, Washington, DC
Politics & Prose, Washington, DC

Daedalus Used Bookshop, Charlottesville, VA
Studio Art Shop, Charlottesville, VA
Williams Corner, Charlottesville, VA

Library Ltd., Clayton, MO
Whistler's Books, Kansas City, MO
Left Bank Books, St. Louis, MO

Paper Skyscraper, Charlotte, NC
Regulator Bookshop, Durham, NC

Chapter Two Bookstore, Charleston, SC
Intermezzo, Columbia, SC
Open Book, Greenville, SC

Square Books, Oxford, MS

Books & Books, Coral Gables, FL
Goerings Book Center, Gainesville, FL
Bookstop, Miami, FL
Rex Art, Miami, FL
Inkwood Books, Tampa, FL

Lenny's News, New Orleans, LA

And at selected Barnes & Noble and Bookstar bookstores nationwide.

Goethe & Weimar

Over 700 brilliant colour prints of objects
displayed at the recently opened Weimar
Classics Exhibition: a sensuous pleasure.
Goethe's times become all the more
vivid through the manifold
explanatory texts from
art and literary history.

1034 pages in 2 volumes
Cloth, smyth sewing
DM 128,–

Stiftung Weimarer Klassik *at Hanser*
www.hanser.de/goethe

EDITIONS & MULTIPLES

VIEWING ROOM OPEN BY APPOINTMENT

LAURIE ANDERSON • VANESSA BEECROFT • ALIGHIERO E BOETTI •

FRANCESCO CLEMENTE • FRANZ GERTSCH • RONI HORN • ALEX KATZ

• ELLSWORTH KELLY • KAREN KILIMNIK • JEFF KOONS • WOLFGANG

LAIB • TRACEY MOFFATT • MALCOLM MORLEY • JUAN MUÑOZ • CADY

NOLAND • JORGE PARDO • RICHARD PRINCE • UGO RONDINONE •

SUSAN ROTHENBERG • THOMAS RUFF • ED RUSCHA • ROMAN SIGNER

• BEAT STREULI • RIRKRIT TIRAVANIJA • LAWRENCE WEINER • FRANZ

WEST and others

CATALOGUE RAISONNÉ: New Catalogue from Parkett exhibition at the
Ludwig Museum, Cologne (60 pages, color reproductions of all one hundred
editions made for Parkett)

Further information on editions, subscriptions and back issues contact:
PARKETT, 155 AVE. OF THE AMERICAS, 2ND FLOOR, NEW YORK, NY 10013
PHONE (212) 673 2660, FAX (212) 271 0704 • WWW. PARKETTART.COM

1999

berlin

2000

artists

visual arts

Katerina VINCOUROVÁ
Rita McBRIDE
Eulàlia VALLDOSERA
Eija-Liisa AHTILA
Willie DOHERTY
Sharon LOCKHART

in

visual arts

Janet CARDIFF
Tacita DEAN
Rodney GRAHAM
Pierre HUYGHE
Ann Veronica JANSSENS
Sophie TOTTIE

literature

residence

Zsófia BALLA
Jeffrey EUGENIDES
Valerie NARBIKOVA
José RIÇO DIREITINHO

literature

László DARVASI
Carlos FRANZ
Einar KÁRASON
Michèle MÉTAIL
Zhai YONG-MING

program

music

Frangis ALI-SADE
Georg Friedrich HAAS
Ronald KUIVILA

music

Ellen FULLMAN
Ed OSBORN
Mario VERANDI

film

Liza JOHNSON
Radim SPACEK
Dimitry TSINTSADZE

film

Hyang-Sook HONG
Franco DE PENA
Lise LABBY-RAVEN

The Artists-in-Residence-Program, *Berliner Künstlerprogramm*, which was initiated in 1963 by the Ford Foundation and taken over by the Deutscher Akademischer Austauschdienst (DAAD) two years later, is a well-known international grant program and an active workshop for artists. It offers between 15 and 20 grants each year in the field of visual arts, literature, music and film. The program defines itself as a forum of artistic dialogue, which is effective and vigorous not only through the work and the presence of the artists living in Berlin, but also through the approximately 100 events a year organized in Berlin, Germany and abroad. Up to date some 1000 artists have been guests in Berlin.

Deutscher Akademischer Austauschdienst – Berliner Künstlerprogramm

Markgrafenstraße 37 • D-10117 Berlin • Fon: ++ 49.30.20 22 080 • Fax: ++ 49.30.20 41 267
e-mail: bkp.berlin@daad.de • www.berlinerkuenstlerprogramm.de

Stop In and Investigate

The Book Sense 76

an eclectic and provocative
selection of the best new books
each month, chosen by the
independent booksellers of
America

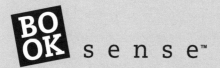

BO OK sense™

Independent Bookstores for Independent Minds

Made in **Taiwan**

CHINA TIMES NOVEL PRIZE WINNER

Notes of a Desolate Man
Chu T'ien-wen
**Translated by Howard Goldblatt
and Sylvia Li-Chun Lin**

This powerful story of gay love and loss echoes Taiwan's precarious existence on the periphery of mainland China.

"A stylish meditation on marginalization, radicalization and decay."
—Susan Salter Reynolds, *Los Angeles Times*

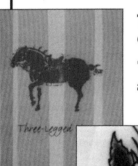

Three-Legged Horse
Cheng Ch'ing-wen

"These 12 tales are the finest examples of modern Chinese fiction I have come across in English." —Bradley Winterton, *South China Morning Post*

Rose, Rose, I Love You
Wang Chen-ho

"Offers several hilarious yet complex dramatizations of attitudes toward Western economic and cultural influence."
—Thomas Hove, *Review of Contemporary Fiction*

MODERN CHINESE LITERATURE FROM TAIWAN

COLUMBIA UNIVERSITY PRESS
columbia.edu/cu/cup   800-944-8648

IMAGES AND SIGNS OF

7 THE 21ST CENTURY hills

Exhibition in the Martin-Gropius-Bau Berlir

www.berlinerfestspiele.de/berlinzweitausen

14 May — 29 October 200c

An Exhibition organized by the Berliner Festspiele